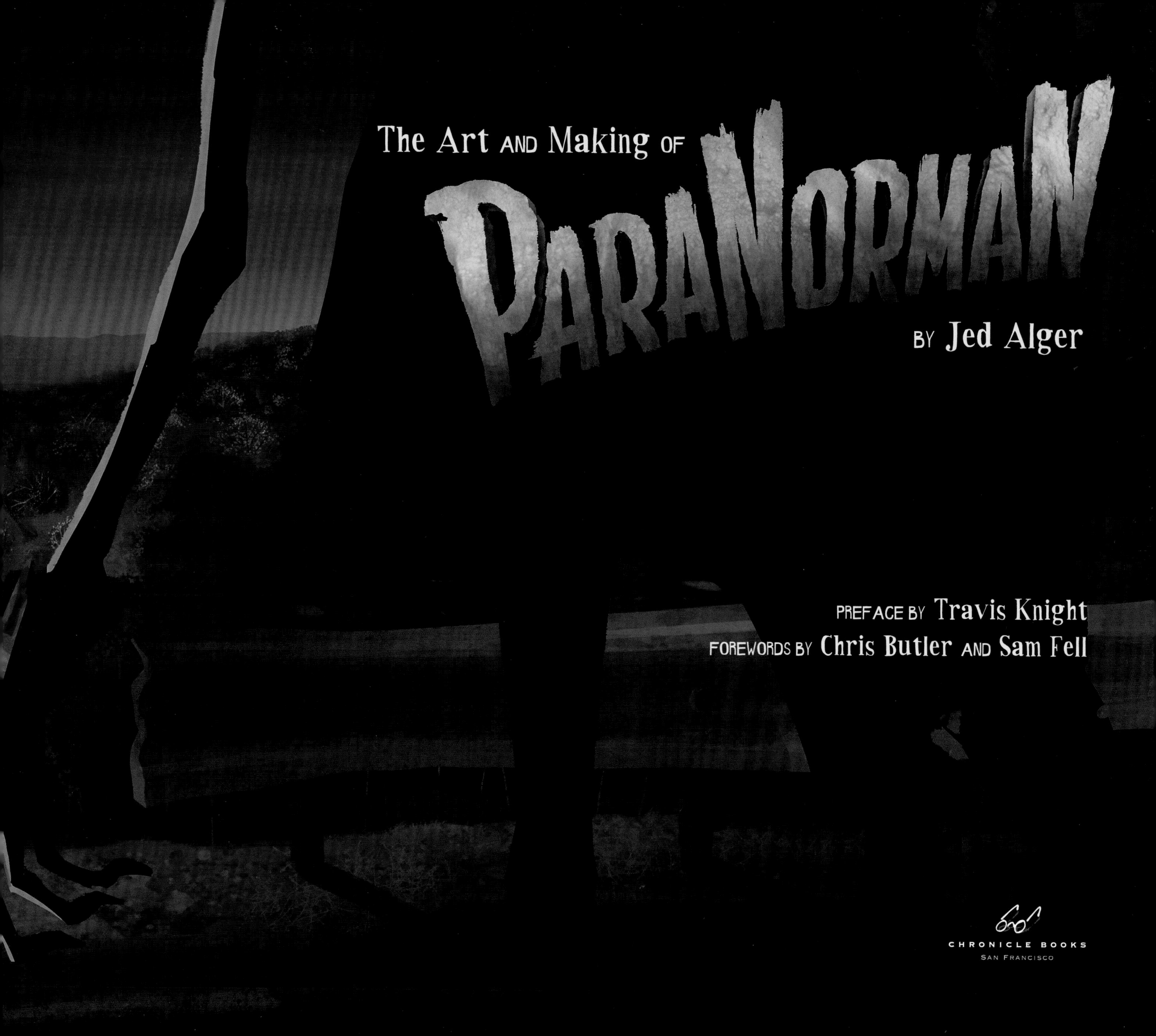

The Art AND Making OF

# ParaNorman

BY Jed Alger

PREFACE BY Travis Knight
FOREWORDS BY Chris Butler AND Sam Fell

CHRONICLE BOOKS
SAN FRANCISCO

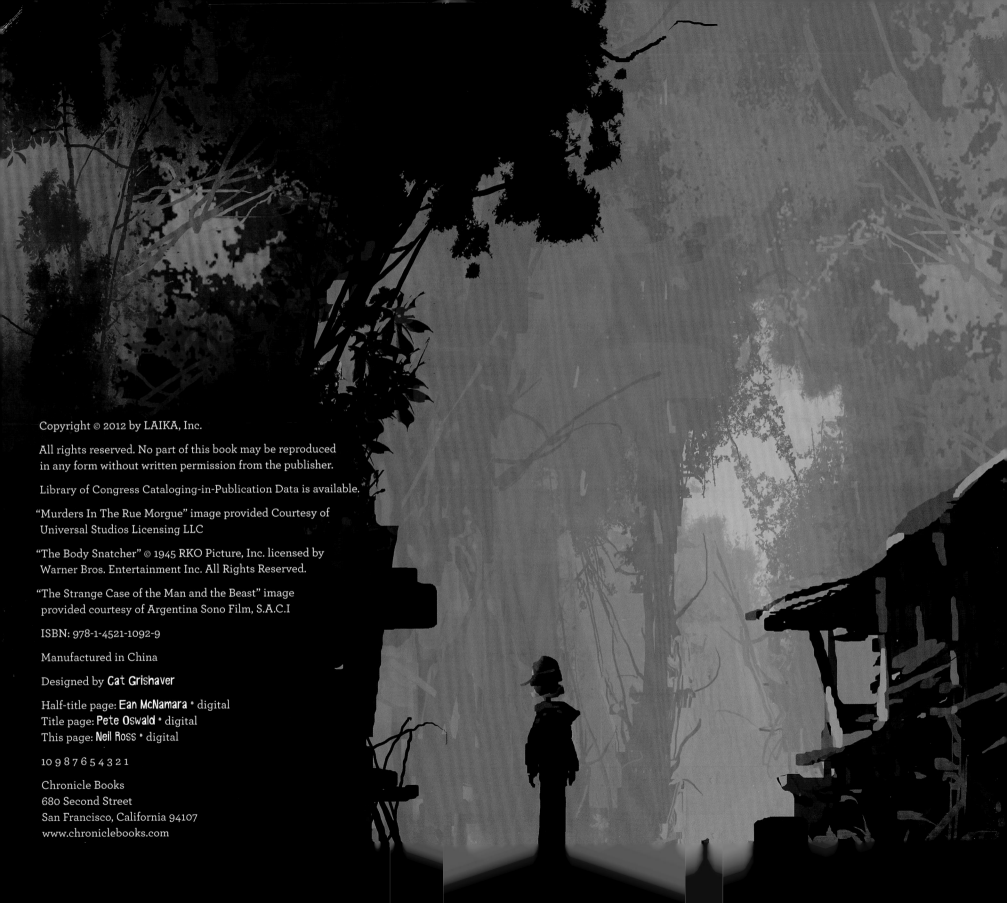

Library of Congress Cataloging-in-Publication Data is available.

"Murders In The Rue Morgue" image provided Courtesy of
Universal Studios Licensing LLC

"The Body Snatcher" © 1945 RKO Picture, Inc. licensed by
Warner Bros. Entertainment Inc. All Rights Reserved.

"The Strange Case of the Man and the Beast" image
provided courtesy of Argentina Sono Film, S.A.C.I

ISBN: 978-1-4521-1092-9

Manufactured in China

Designed by Cat Grishaver

Half-title page: Ean McNamara • digital
Title page: Pete Oswald • digital
This page: Neil Ross • digital

10 9 8 7 6 5 4 3 2 1

Chronicle Books
680 Second Street
San Francisco, California 94107
www.chroniclebooks.com

# Contents

Chris Butler • pencil

# Confessions of a Cave Dweller

**I** AM A CAVEMAN. A thickheaded, knuckle-dragging troglodyte who refuses to evolve with the times.

There, I said it. After all, I live in an era of glossy, high-tech digital perfection, and I work with a pair of decidedly low-tech hands. You see, I'm a stop-motion animator, practitioner of that most anachronistic of art forms that cherishes craft over technology. And while technology is a triumph of organized, disciplined intellect, stop-motion is an exercise in messy, physical exertion. It's hard to imagine two perspectives more at odds with each other. But one of the things that make LAIKA unique is how we fuse the sensibilities of Luddites and technophiles, merging the handmade warmth and charm of stop-motion with the precision and flexibility of cutting-edge technology to create something entirely new.

It was the approach we took on our film *Coraline*, and an approach we continue to pursue, to push the medium to its breaking point and beyond in order to tell bold, distinctive, and enduring stories. After *Coraline*, the question was, what would be the groundbreaking idea to take LAIKA and the medium to the next evolutionary stage? The answer came in the form of a quiet, charming, and perplexingly humble story artist named Chris Butler.

Nearing the end of production on *Coraline*, Chris, our head of story, approached us with an idea that had been roiling around in his head for a while. It was the story of an exceedingly strange boy, who ultimately uses his remarkable gifts to save the very people who marginalized him. It was a moving and human story, one of intense beauty and emotional truth. And zombies.

Groaning, slobbering, foot-dragging zombies. For me, a guy who grew up subsisting on a pop-culture diet of Ray Harryhausen's spasmodic stop-motion marvels and George Romero's shambling, brain-eating ghouls, it was a dream project.

It should be noted, by the way, that Chris Butler is an artistic dynamo. An exceptional draftsman, world-class storyteller, and a virtuoso with language, his work is sheer poetry. Chris is so damned talented it's almost unseemly. He, together with his similarly and enviably skilled directing partner, Sam Fell, led and inspired a motley collection of consummate artists and technicians, steely-eyed pragmatists and starry-eyed dreamers, devoted entirely to pouring their souls into this wonderful story.

In an odd way, the story of *ParaNorman* is largely the story of the people who made it. Because look, let's face it, artists in general, and animators in particular, are strange people. In high school, we were the kids who got shoved into our gym lockers. Who holed up in our parents' basements, rocking out to Rush albums and rolling polyhedral dice in the latest Gary Gygax D&D module. And as grownups, well, we play with dolls for a living. Clearly not a lot of growth there.

What's more, the life of a stop-motion animator is hardly the most socially enriching existence. We spend most of our days with minimal human contact, stuffed away in a dark cave surrounded by giant Duvetyne curtains, sweating under hot set lights, and inhaling noxious fumes from rubber cement and hot glue. It's perhaps no wonder that we're essentially a band of oddball, navel-gazing mole people with limited social graces.

But there's also something quite wonderful and liberating about living on the fringes of society. Like our hero Norman, we are given a peculiar perspective on the world. You think beyond your own experiences. You become in tune with things that others may have forgotten. Childlike things. And, if you're lucky, you're possessed of the uncanny ability to peer through the scrim of everyday existence to find beauty and magic in the ordinary. As it happens, these are defining qualities of the prodigiously gifted crew of *ParaNorman*.

These pages are a celebration of the misfits, the outcasts, the beautiful freaks who see the world in a different way and, in the process, enrich the lives of those around them. We're all the better for it. Hopefully, like me, you'll be moved and inspired by their stories, their imagination, their brilliant artistry. And you'll be reminded of that time-honored truism: You don't become extraordinary by being normal.

Here's to being weird.

Cheers,

# TRAVIS KNIGHT
## President and CEO, LAIKA

## BY CHRIS BUTLER,
### writer and director

**T**HIS BOOK IS ESSENTIALLY THE EQUIVALENT OF me cornering you at a party and forcing you to look at baby pictures. You won't get any apologies, however, because I'm a ridiculously proud parent. *ParaNorman* is my baby and it has been kicking and screaming and soiling its diapers in my head for many years. Now that it is taking its first tentative steps into the wider world, I can use this opportunity to coo affectionately about its conception.

A family legend, expounded by my dear departed Nanna, suggested that I was born with a pencil in my hand. As gynecologically unpleasant as this sounds for my mother, and as much as it might explain why she had no more children after me, it is as succinct and perfect a summation as I can think of for my innate ability to draw stuff. I apparently had a "gift."

Like so many children with an artistic predilection, I was also something of an outcast. I didn't fit in. I discovered that standing out from the crowd was only an option if the crowd got to call me names and throw things at me. When grown-ups used to tell me, "My school years were the best years of my life!" I used to think, "Wow, your lives must *really* suck."

And so I kept myself to myself. I read a lot. I drew even more. I dined out on a diet of monster movies and animated TV shows and comic books that presented me with all manner of colorful abstractions of the decidedly less rewarding real world.

This is where ParaNorman came from. It's the story of a lonely, bullied, gifted kid existing in a world that's something like what might happen if John Carpenter and John Hughes made an episode of Scooby Doo together.

It is a movie that celebrates "the different," not just narratively, but artistically, as does the studio that produced it. LAIKA is a bubbling crucible of every kind of abnormally talented dork, nerd, freak, and geek you could ever have the good fortune to meet. One of them is my boss, and a source of endless inspiration, the phenomenally talented Travis Knight. He not only liked my script, but stood behind it and championed it as an ambitious and irreverent vision never diminished by compromise. For that I'll be forever grateful.

This book aims to illustrate the artistry in our medium, but also in our process: in our day-to-day rituals, banter, notes, and doodles. It's not only a testament to Sam Fell and Arianne Sutner and all the heads of departments mentioned in these pages, but to all the guys who stand behind them. There are hundreds of them, each equally deserving of praise and recognition for what they've brought to this project. This is the most exceptional crew I've ever worked with. It's been a privilege to trust them with my baby's upbringing.

One day in the future, when ParaNorman has all grown up and moved on and never calls or writes or comes home for Christmas any more, I'll still remember all of this with affection, pride, and awe. This experience has been a true gift.

I STARTED OUT MY CAREER as a stop-frame director/animator at the beginning of the '90s. I loved the magic in having real objects come to life, but by the time I got to make my first feature film, the medium had become frustrating. The amount of all the post-production work I would have needed to get even close to my vision for the film made CG a much more viable option. That was it . . . bye-bye stop frame.

On my return I found that LAIKA had led a revolution in stop-frame features with their production *Coraline*. They advanced the medium so far in such a short time I felt like a kind of Rip Van Winkle coming upon a familiar yet incomparable world. The way they had integrated visual effects and rapid prototype technology into traditional stop-frame production was completely liberating. It was an amazing, unique machine, and with *ParaNorman* they were ready to drive it into a new direction.

Chris's script had some delicate emotional scenes, some epic visuals, and some funny social satire in it too. I thought it read more like a live action script which rhymed with me because I had been thinking a lot about shooting live action movies at the time. In comparison a lot of stop-frame felt old-fashioned and a bit stilted in its camera and editing. Both of us wanted to get away from the medium's roots in puppet theater and find a fresh approach. We wanted to shoot scope and spectacle like a big live action effects movie and to observe the real world in subtle and nuanced detail like a cool indie

drama. Every department would have to find new techniques and approaches to accommodate. We asked for the characters' skin to have color variations and some translucency so the light would react more delicately. We wanted to shoot extreme close-ups so we needed more detail from models and puppets. We felt the animation needed to be 'real' and subtle—actually have the characters think and feel like people, not *act* theatrically. Mob scenes should feel truly big and threatening. As we pushed forward on all fronts with our madly ambitious and precise vision for the movie we were waiting to be told we were asking too much . . . but in fact they gave us more. This fabulous band of high- and low-tech artists consistently delivered the most amazing, generous, subtle, incredibly inventive work imaginable.

But there's more to come. LAIKA's vision for the medium of stop-frame has really just begun to unfold. It's impossible to tell exactly where they will take us in the future but I know they will amaze and entertain audiences for many years to come.

# chapter 1

# Welcome to LAIKA

### The Birthplace of *ParaNorman*

**T**HE FIRST THING TO KNOW about making a stop-motion film is: collaboration. It's just too big and too unwieldy to belong to one person. The writer helps the art director, who helps the character designer, who both influences and is influenced by the story department, and on and on. The directors talk to every-one, of course, and in the case of *ParaNorman*, this is a team of directors—Sam Fell and Chris Butler. The directors' vision unites the film, but that vision is com-municated to and interpreted by LAIKA's 300-odd (and in some cases, very odd) artists, craftspeople, engineers, model makers, tailors, woodworkers, and problem solvers, each of whom puts a bit of him- or herself into the work.

It's an amazing, complex, sometimes arcane process, seemingly far removed from the more showy technical wizardry of modern cinema. But if you automatically associate stop-motion film making with a quaint method of story-telling, you have not spent any time at LAIKA. "Stop-motion" says Travis Knight, CEO of LAIKA and one of its chief animators, "is a medium with its own language and its own particular set of storytelling tools with which we can tackle any genre—comedy, tragedy, horror, drama. The whole idea of LAIKA is to create a place where all these talented people can come together and make something that couldn't be made any other way." If that means combing through dumpsters looking for the right piece of scrap, so be it. Likewise if it means employing the cutting edge in computer 3D graphic effects, bring it on. There is a powerful love of stop-motion at LAIKA, but it stops short of reverence. These people are not building a shrine to stop-motion film making, they are bringing it into the future.

## The Writer

**EVERYTHING STARTS WITH AN IDEA AND,** as it happens, this idea started with Chris Butler. He'd been thinking about a particular story for a few years, quite a few years actually, just kicking it around. It was all about childhood and the perils of growing up and what happens when you know a secret but no one quite believes you . . . oh, and zombies. When it became clear the idea wasn't going to play nice and go away, Butler started writing it down. What resulted was the remarkable tale of Norman Babcock, a perfectly average kid who happens to be able to talk with ghosts, a talent for which he is bullied daily. But it is also the only thing that will save his town, the old New England burg of Blithe Hollow, from a 300-year-old curse.

Norman doesn't do it alone, of course. Mr. Prenderghast, Norman's estranged uncle and a fairly eccentric character around town, tries to warn Norman about the curse. Unfortunately, the fact that Mr. P. dies and has to deliver his warning from beyond the grave complicates things. So when Norman tries to spread the alarm, he faces a credibility gap. The first people to believe him are fellow misfits Salma and Neil. Next Neil's brother, the strapping jock Mitch, gets roped in, largely because he has a vehicle, a panel van he dotes on. Courtney, Norman's incredulous sister, gets on board strictly out of interest in Mitch. And even Alvin, the prototypical school bully, joins the team, as more and more supernatural forces begin to shake the community. When the adults of the town begin to panic, it is this crew of kids who takes control and saves the day, despite a septet of very active zombies, a roaring lynch mob, and some extremely powerful paranormal turmoil.

*"I wanted ParaNorman to address the kinds of issues that really affect us when we're growing up: bullying, fitting in, the formation of identity, and, of course, zombie invasion. "*
—CHRIS BUTLER, director

Butler feels that he more or less grew up with this idea in his head. "As a kid in England, I watched a lot of TV, and a lot of *American* TV, and that really influenced me. I loved *Scooby Doo* and I wanted *ParaNorman* to feel like, you know, what if Scooby Doo were real?" His script reads like it was written by an aficionado not just of Scooby, but also the *Brady Bunch* and midnight creature features. It is a rich brew of symbols and allusions that seems to connect with people at an almost pre-conscious level.

At the time he was working on the script, Butler was working as head of story and character design on LAIKA's first stop-motion feature, *Coraline*, so he showed an early draft of *ParaNorman* to LAIKA CEO Travis Knight. The story was chock full of red flags—so many characters, lots of crowd scenes, ghosts, and some intense special effects—none of which comes easily to stop-motion because of technical challenges. A lot of characters means a lot of model design and construction, which is expensive; it means more elaborate sets to hold all these characters and, especially, it means a lot of work for the animators. Floating ghosts require more rigging and present some special animation challenges. And special effects? Stop-motion ceded its mantle as a viable special effects medium a generation ago, yielding to the CG (Computer Graphics) juggernaut in the early nineties. But despite the challenges—or really because of them—LAIKA took the project on. Says Knight, "LAIKA is all about pushing stop-motion film into new areas, finding new ways to keep it fresh. With *Coraline*, we took it to a new level. And with this script we saw the opportunity to go even further. We had to do this movie."

And with that decision, the process of turning this script into a feature-length stop-frame film was set into motion—a process that would ultimately consume more than three years of intense creative effort from a huge team of people, a process built of art and craft and science, a process so complex its best comparisons are with the space program, at one end of the technological scale, and with the building of ancient cathedrals at the other. A stop-motion film is always a brave undertaking; *ParaNorman*, with its expansive cast and genre-busting special effects, promised to take the art form to a new place.

Chris Butler • digital

13

"I'm basically Norman. When I was eleven I had big soulful eyes, was painfully shy, got picked on at school, and had an unfeasibly large head. There's still some debate in my family as to whether or not I can actually talk to ghosts."
—CHRIS BUTLER

Neil asks Jackson about his 'gift'. They go to Neil's garden so he can speak to his dead dog Philbert.

'Can toff feel me if I pet him?'

'Sure.'

'Oh.... that's not his chin.'

Chris Butler * pencil

Chris Butler * ink

Chris Butler * ink

SEQ 1000

Julian Narino * pencil

SEQ 1200

Julian Narino * pencil

"We couldn't just copy real life. That just ends up feeling lifeless and creepy. We had to find our own kind of offbeat naturalism, from storyboards to animation to camera, effects, and sound."
—SAM FELL, director

Chris Butler • pencil

15

# THE
## Story Department

JUST OFF HIGHWAY 26, between the charm of Portland and the splendor of the Oregon coast, there is a giant warehouselike building—you couldn't call it the ugliest building in the world, only because there are a lot of ugly buildings in office parks, but it would be fair to call it nondescript. No sign out front. No name over the door. In fact, it's a bit of a challenge just finding the door. But let's say you do find the door, and you go in and make your way through a generic lobby and up a set of carpeted stairs. Now you're in a long, open room, quiet as a library, where ten artists are sketching on digital tablets.

Their job is to turn the script into a detailed set of storyboards, which capture all the nuance the script merely implies. Working closely with the directors, they take the first pass at blocking out a shot-by-shot, and sometimes moment-by-moment, reel of the film.

"The storyboard," says artist Graham Annable, "is the blueprint for the film. We take the script and we transform it into something visual. The fun and scary thing about doing what we do is, we don't know what we're going to get out of those pages. You learn early on that what works in the written script doesn't translate the way you think it will when you turn it into images. Sometimes it comes out better than you'd hoped. Sometimes it just doesn't work and then we have to interpret and invent—which can be a fun part of the job."

It is the peculiar nature of stop-motion that makes this process so absolutely critical. Every single thing that happens—every smile, every reaction, every seemingly serendipitous moment—must be imagined and then created *before* filming begins. Needless to say, this process is a journey full of experimentation and adjustment, and the animation stage is a terrible place for experimentation: Stage work is too meticulous, too time-consuming and, hence, far too expensive for trial and error. Storyboards are the perfect way to mount an exploration of the script.

"Each storyboard artist will take a sequence, maybe four to eight pages of the script," says Annable. "We sit with it. Think about it. Then we start drawing. As we progress, our drawings will get more detailed—we'll start incorporating character design and set design—but those early drawings are fast, almost stick figures. It's just intended to get the film up and going." In this early stage, the storyboard artists are intuiting what's between the lines of the script. "It's my favorite part," Annable says. "It's like fresh snow and we just get to dive in and play."

> ## "You make a stop-motion film twice—first in story, with drawings. Then you make it for real."
> ## —CHRIS BUTLER

Storyboarding a sequence might require four- to eight-hundred individual drawings, depending on the level of detail and action in the script. "And that's just what goes into editorial," Annable adds. "All the experimentation and playing around never gets that far." Once it goes into editorial, the directors get a look at it and make their comments. Then the editor starts adding sound and voices. "That gives the storyboard a whole new dimension," Annable explains, "which usually leads to another round of changes. Some sections we'll board over and over and over again. Some are pretty good after just a few rounds. You never know."

"In the end, our job is to make the story as fun and compelling as possible. We know we'll sometimes draw something and the animators will say, 'This just isn't physically possible.' But if we were always focused on what physically works and lost sight of the story, we wouldn't be doing our job."

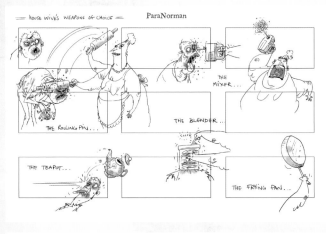

18

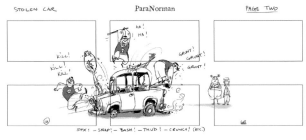

**Mike Smith** • pencil

"When my script first got the go-ahead, I went back to my office and after quietly hugging my knees and rocking on my chair for a day or two, I got right into what I know, and I storyboarded out the first five or six pages of script. Then I slapped it together in an extremely rough cut with temp music and scratch dialogue, and I stared at it for a while, and I thought, 'This is going to work.' "
—CHRIS BUTLER

**Pete Oswald** • digital

Ean McNamara • digital

Dave Vandervoort • digital

19

"Some animated movies want to transport you to a fantasy world or another time. *ParaNorman* needed a different philosophy. It didn't make sense for the film to feel like it was conjured up by designers tucked away in a studio. We needed to be 'of' the contemporary world; exploring mundane reality and reporting on it. There's just something fundamentally cool about seeing the world you live in observed in miniature."
—SAM FELL

Ross Stewart • digital

Pete Oswald • digital

22

# THE Edit Suite

The room feels a bit like a teenager's bedroom—windowless, a little dank, filled with electronics, a comfy couch, and a couple mismatched chairs—except instead of a rumpled bed, there is a desk with a couple of large monitors and a stack of computer gear. Christopher Murrie, *ParaNorman*'s editor, works the controls as the directors, Butler and Fell, watch what he's serving up on a flat-screen TV mounted opposite the couch.

Generally, we think of the editorial process as coming at the end of a film's production cycle. The cameras have wrapped, the dust has settled, and now the editor hunkers down to cut something together for the director out of the dozens if not hundreds of hours of footage—takes, retakes, reverse-angles, wide coverage, and anything else the director thought to shoot. Not so for animation: You use the storyboards to figure out exactly what you want to shoot. And you use the editor to figure out how the storyboards work.

"Editing is not a postproduction process in a stop-motion film," Chris explains. "I'm on from start to finish. If anything, preproduction is my busiest time." The storyboard artists send Chris their frames in the form of jpegs, digital files he can load into his computer. Meanwhile, Chris has organized a table read of the script. "I'll get eight or ten people and we'll read through the script while I record it. We try all sorts of approaches to lines, trial reads; we just explore." He then takes that *scratch track* and the jpegs and he starts cutting together a rough version of the film. The directors take a look and give him feedback. The storyboard artists make revisions. Meanwhile, the character designs are progressing and this progress starts to show up in the new boards, which go back to Chris in editorial.

At some point in the process, the scratch track is replaced by a new recording from local amateur actors, and this sharper read begins to inform the cut. Later, Chris will get the final voice track from the professional talent. "They bring a lot of nuance and energy to the script. Things we maybe didn't know were there. That's a huge step forward. After that I might spend a couple days just editing sound, not even looking at picture, until the story sounds right. Then I might turn the sound off and just edit picture for a couple days."

"We revise storyboards so frequently in the beginning," Murrie says. "I'll get storyboards and two days later we'll have a cut and I'll show it to the directors and we'll change things and that loop goes around and around and around. All the while, I'll start taking boards and cutting them up and putting them together—combining angles, widening a shot. I become an adjunct to the story department, I get to play cinematographer, I get to play director a little. We might cut the whole film two or three times over before we start shooting, which is fantastic for an editor. You get to cut the film you want to make. You aren't stuck with any poorly planned shots. If I want the coverage, I just ask for it to be drawn."

This freedom and power also has a daunting side: The only limit to what goes into this film is what the editor, the directors, the writers, and the storyboard artists are able to create. "Of course, you don't have the happy accidents you get in live-action, the unexpected look from an actor or maybe an actor lingers on a line longer in one take. You don't get that," Chris says. "So you have to always be imagining into the drawing. The story artists bring a lot of amazing stuff to the table but you know there's always going to be a whole realm of possibility beyond that. So you're looking at what you have and imagining into it, into where you want it to go."

The editorial suite comes to resemble a kind of dark, high-tech Mt. Olympus, with directors Fell and Butler in near-permanent residence. Here they are able to pull up on screen all the work in progress—storyboards at first, then, as things get rolling, everything from facial animations to the design of a particular character's eyeball, to finished shots. Chris Butler has said there are four million decisions to be made in a stop-motion film and, while he may have been underestimating, a huge number of them happen in this room. For the next three years a seemingly endless parade of animators, designers, set dressers, model makers, special effects wizards, and so on, come in, sit with the directors for feedback, and go back out to make it happen.

Meanwhile, elsewhere in this cavernous building, the intensive work of character design and art direction—the "look" of the film—is progressing full-tilt.

Vintage horror movie posters inspired the mock posters on Norman's bedroom walls.

Dave Vandervoort • digital

> "In live-action, editing is a reductive process. The director goes and shoots all this footage, gives it to the editor, and they cut a ninety-minute film from it. Stop-motion is purely additive. You start with nothing."
> —CHRISTOPHER MURRIE

Ean McNamara • digital

Heidi Smith • digital

Kevin Dart • digital

Pete Oswald • digital

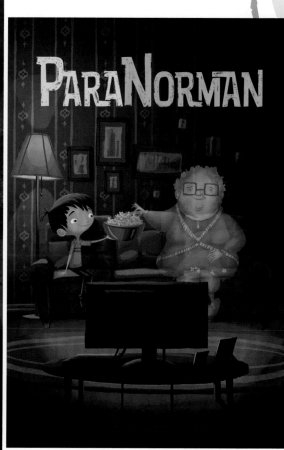

Chris Turnham • digital

# chapter 2

# Giving the Film Characters

> The journey from idea to physical puppet

29
☠

Heidi Smith · pencil

# WHERE  Characters COME FROM

To MAKE A MOVIE IS TO MAKE DECISIONS, big and little. What happens, where does it happen, to whom is it happening, but also what's the atmosphere, what colors are in play, how does the heroine wear her hair? This decision making is there in any movie, of course, but a stop-motion film takes it to an unparalleled extreme because every single thing must be made and animated by hand. A live-action director who sets his film in New England can count on New England landscapes and New England lighting—they are provided free, and the director simply needs to decide how to best take advantage of what nature has provided.

In a stop-motion film all this will have to be built, and built to the specifications of the directors and their team. It's a godlike level of control, and nowhere is this more obvious than in the character design process. The players, who so far have existed as ideas in the writer's head and words on the pages of the script, then as rough sketches—sometimes ridiculously rough—in the developing storyboards, need to solidify into real, corporeal beings.

Given Chris Butler's background as a storyboard artist and his skills as a draftsman, it is no surprise that he had some initial ideas about character design to bring to the table as *ParaNorman* went into development. The next step was to explore these ideas, to pursue them and push them until they sparkled or until they broke and some new idea could emerge from the rubble. To this end, Butler approached some fairly established 2-D artists whose work had particularly impressed and inspired him. Butler had been awed by the mood and menace of *The Secret of Kells*, so he tapped the talent of *Kell*'s director/writer/character designer Tom Moore and *Kell*'s art director, Ross Stewart, to help him with *ParaNorman*. In a totally different vein, the much-acclaimed graphic illustrator Guy Davis was also engaged to help develop these characters. And while it might be difficult to point to specific artifacts of these explorations in the final character designs, the process was incredibly valuable and fruitful in that it opened up the horizons of what a character in this film could look like, far beyond Butler's early imaginings.

In the end, after these seasoned veterans had had their go at it, it was a young, untested illustrator named Heidi Smith, with nary a film credit to her name, who ended up capturing the essence of the eclectic bunch of characters who populate *ParaNorman*.

The choice of such a relatively inexperienced illustrator to drive the crucial process of character design is not without risk. But when Butler saw Heidi's work, there was an immediate connection and almost a sense of recognition, as if here were the characters he'd been writing about all these years. He saw in Heidi's drawings a kind of energy—what came to be dubbed a "nervous quality of line"—that seemed to bring an inner life to these drawings.

In a small, windowless, well-lit work space adjacent to the storyboard department, Smith goes at her drawings with a ragged intensity, going through box after box of the green 6B pencils she uses exclusively. She sharpens the pencils by hand with an X-ACTO knife until the point is as sharp as a weapon. In fact a Heidi Smith pencil looks like it could be a prop from the movie— hand-crafted, familiar, but somewhat off in its proportions: the *idea* of a pencil.

Her work space is cluttered with bodies and body parts, drawings of them—a skull here, an arm here, an eye peeking out from underneath a sketch of a zombie—all rendered in that characteristic line. She holds the pencil well up the barrel and stands back from the page as if she is both creating and observing at the same time. Some characters come easily, she says. Others, like Courtney, were harder. "I drew Courtney over and over and over. I hated it. I couldn't get it right. And then, it just happened. I hated Courtney. And now I love her."

"Heidi's work is so well observed, but so radical, unhinged, messy, brutally honest. It informed everything that came after."
—SAM FELL

> "I went through portfolios of all these young artists and then, you come across one portfolio that doesn't fit with the rest, doesn't follow the trends in that school or in animation; they do their own thing because they are good at it. That's Heidi."
> —CHRIS BUTLER

Despite being tucked away upstairs, in the quietest backwater of the quietest part of the LAIKA building, Heidi has further barricaded herself behind a kind of phalanx of rice paper screens. Within these confines the feeling is that of monkish seclusion, a feeling Heidi augments by working with headphones on.

To prepare for the job, Smith looked at the script and then dove in. "Chris didn't want me to have too much information. He wanted to see what I would do." What she did was to pull from a range of influences. One character reminds her of a pirate. Another of a character from an old rock poster from her brother's bedroom. It is an entirely personal world, one in which a zombie might be lovable, and a cheerleader something of a villain.

Bit by bit, line by line, the characters of Butler's script were taking shape at the end of Heidi Smith's 6B pencil. But the next step is where the process begins its radical departure from conventional animation and steps inexorably into the tangible, physical world of stop-motion filmmaking.

Heidi Smith · pencil

PERRY GUY EXPRESSIONS

DEAD JUDGE EXPRESSIONS

32

Dave Vandervoort • pencil  Deanna Marsigliese • pencil

Dave Vandervoort • pencil  Deanna Marsigliese • pencil

"When I draw and I think about design, it becomes a disaster. Once I start trying to be careful, I might as well throw away the drawing. It has to be emotional, it has to be raw. It has to be rough. That's where the character is."
—HEIDI SMITH

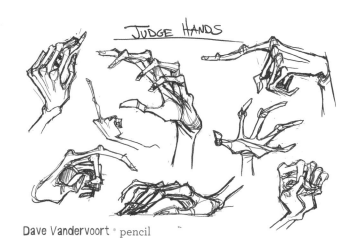

JUDGE HANDS

Dave Vandervoort • pencil

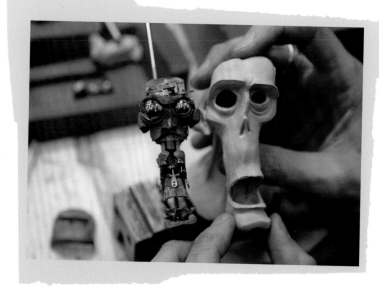

Heidi Smith • pencil

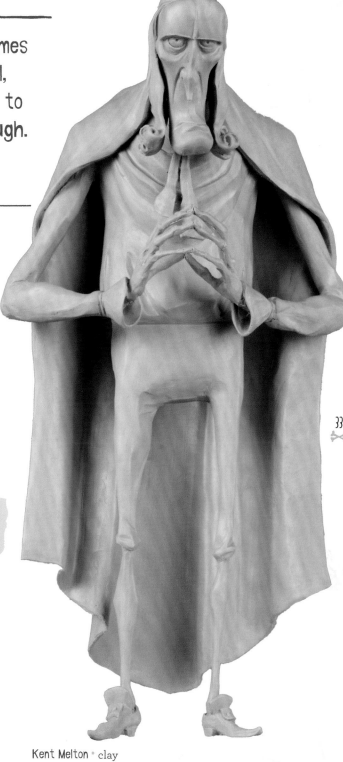

Kent Melton • clay

33

"I had very specific ideas in my head of who these characters were, long before the project ever started. When Heidi came along and started drawing them, some of them came uncannily close. She not only drew people that I recognized, but she also drew people that everyone recognizes. You see her first design for Perry and you say, "Yes, I've met that guy, and yes, he's such an asshole."

—CHRIS BUTLER

Heidi Smith • pencil

Chris Butler and Trevor Dalmer • digital and digital paint

Kevin Dart • digital

Heidi Smith and Trevor Dalmer • pencil and digital paint

Ean McNamara • digital

Heidi Smith and Ean McNamara • pencil and digital paint

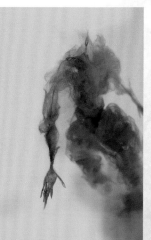

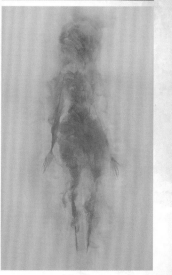

37

Ean McNamara • digital

Nelson Lowry • digital

FAVORITE

Kevin Dart • pencil

Heidi Smith • pencil

38

Chris Butler • digital

Chris Butler and Heidi Smith • digital

"When I draw something it's an intense experience,
which is why I get neurotic about my privacy.
I need that. I have to become like the character.
It's like acting. I have to jump into the paper and
try to be that character."
—HEIDI SMITH

Kent Melton • clay

THE
## Maquette

**N**OW WE LEAVE HEIDI SMITH'S HIDEAWAY, past the storyboard department and down the stairs, moving through the afterthought of a reception area, decked out in standard-issue corporate, and within a few paces we enter the heart of LAIKA, a high-ceilinged complex of interconnected workshops, densely populated with artists and artisans of all sorts. Here there are rows of workstations that bear no relation to the beige cubicles that the term typically conjures up. These are busy, workmanlike areas lined with tools and artifacts of the trade—arms, legs, lumps of clay, here a set of wire clippers of different sizes, here a vise, here the hose of a dust collector descending over a workbench. The air is crisp, there is the smell of freshly cut wood, a radio is playing somewhere and, all around you, people are bent to their work—you are reminded that stop-motion is a physical art that takes place in three dimensions. Things are being built.

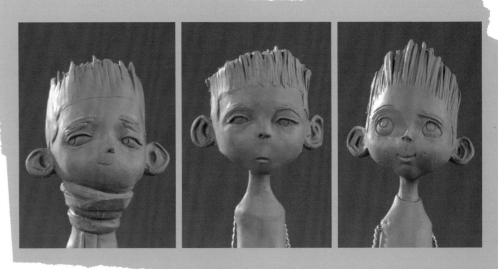

In one of these stations, sculptor Kent Melton is applying clay to the head of a zombie, a rather imposing-looking character whose sharp, exaggerated features are so riveting it takes you a moment to notice the broken ribs protruding from his rotted vestments, revealing a gaping body cavity. Kent is a striking man, bearded, somehow both spritely and grave—he reminds one of Herr Drosselmeyer, the toymaker from *The Nutcracker*—fittingly, because Melton's job is to take a drawing and bring it to life, imagining the leap from flat art to physical puppet, a scale model of the character called a *maquette*. In the small, interconnected world of stop-motion filmmaking there is, arguably, no one better at making maquettes than Kent Melton.

Modern humans are so well trained at seeing the depth in two-dimensional images—photos, paintings, films—that this job may seem a simple one. However, tackle the practical task of making a 3-D model from a 2-D drawing and you will quickly discover how much crucial information is simply missing. Bridging the gap is an act of imagination that requires Melton to make assumptions about the inner character—how does he or she move? Morose or energetic? Boundless or controlled? Angry and bold or sinister and timid?

And here is where the collaboration between designer and sculptor—between the young, brash newcomer Heidi Smith and the courtly, inventive veteran Melton—becomes so crucial. Smith's drawings, so immediate and impressionistic, certainly leave a lot of physical detail to Melton's imagination. But the energy is in there, the character is in there, and that's the important part.

"I would go upstairs to Heidi's sanctuary," Melton recalls, "and she'd be hidden away behind those screens with her headphones on, so I'd just knock on the screen and make her talk to me. I wanted to know what she was thinking so I could make that part of my thinking."

When Melton gets to work on a character, he dives in. He has read the script, he has talked with Heidi, he has the drawing in front of him, and off he goes, working extremely quickly, almost before he can think too much.

Kent Melton * clay

The first step is a frame—an inner skeleton of wire—in which Melton tries to capture the energy of the character: its posture, its bearing, and its attitude. Then comes the clay.

Melton first learned to sculpt in wood, a much more dense medium that requires greater physical effort (he likens it to practicing for clay with weights on his wrists). The result is that he is a habitual over-sculptor, making bold moves, cutting away and then adding back. Clamped to his desk, alongside the typical cutting and modeling tools, there is a hand-cranked pasta machine at the ready. Melton flattens a small piece of clay and with a wire-ended tool begins deftly working it into a ragged tangle that becomes the Judge's ghostly tresses.

SKULL

NEUTRAL

1.

2.

3.

42

4.

5.

6.

7.

8.

9.

> "This is the quickest I've seen a cast of characters come together. There's something special from Heidi's drawings to Kent's sculpting and then out to the rest of the team—it's been amazing."
> —SAM FELL

Depending on the complexity of the character, Melton can generally create a model in about four days. He then shares this work with his collaborators—Heidi Smith; Georgina Hayns, head of the puppet department; and, of course, the directors, Fell and Butler—who give him feedback, sometimes of a general nature, sometimes of incredible precision.

For the directors, who at this point are moving between storyboards, character design, and art direction, it becomes a feat of mental magic to keep the details straight, but there they are, checking in with a hand sculptor on the minutiae of exactly where and how thick the pad of flesh beneath the thumb should be and what happens when you add tiny fingerless gloves, before moving on to look briefly at a sample of hair for Norman, then arriving at Kent's area to see what's become of his zombie. Georgina Hayns joins them here and you know this sculpt is in good shape because the conversation quickly turns to its shoe and just how thick it should be, with how much of a curl at the toe. Melton can breathe a sigh of relief. A change in story, a revelation about the character's role, even a little bit of unforeseen action might require some rethinking of his form, but for the moment, as far as this particular zombie goes, Melton's work is done and done well.

44

Ben Adams • clay

Kent Melton • clay

Nelson Lowry • digital

# Face Facts

## How RP technology has raised the stop-motion bar

**T**HERE ARE THREE WAYS TO ANIMATE A FACE in stop-motion: LAIKA's trademarked form of clay animation, Claymation®, where you shape clay in increments to get the expression you want; *mechanical head*, where a silicone skin is stretched over a complex of gears and paddles that the animator manipulates to change the shape of the face; and *replacement face animation*, which is just what it sounds like.

Replacement face animation can be incredibly simple. But to do real animation—to show emotion and reaction moving across the character's face—you need a lot of replacement faces which, traditionally, has been a time-consuming and expensive process due to all the sculpting and painting involved. This is where Rapid Prototype technology, or RP, comes in and it's here as much as anywhere that LAIKA is steadily, quietly revolutionizing stop-motion filmmaking.

Immediately adjacent to the bright, high-ceilinged workshops of the puppet department, but a world away from the convivial, collegial hustle and bustle of that environment, in a long, hushed, dimly lit room, digital artists swim in the glow of their monitors, intent on their work. This is LAIKA's Rapid Prototype department, led by Brian McLean. Brian grew up on stop-motion: He was a big fan of the California Raisins and of the animated *Adventures of Mark Twain*; in fact, he spent many hours carving his versions of Mr. Twain and Huck and Tom from plasticine. And let's not forget his sixth-grade science project on stop-motion entitled "The Principle of the Persistence of Vision." Brian loved stop-motion.

47

> "The 3-D printer really bridges the practical, hands-on side with the technical side. The computer is a tool and the printer is a bridge between the tool and the real world."
> —BRIAN McLEAN

Brian McLean and Tory Bryant compare Norman's painted maquette to the digital paint map.

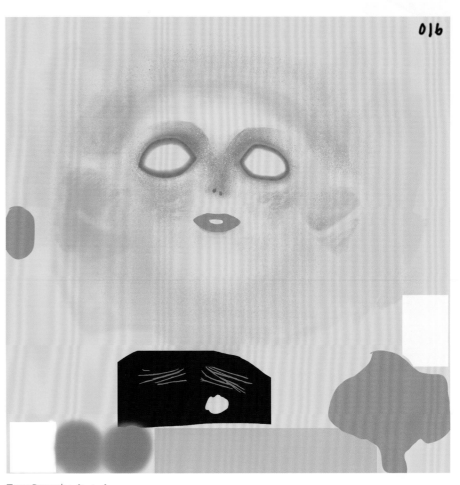

016

Tory Bryant · digital

But Brian also had a penchant for technology. He was teaching sculpture at the California College of Arts and Crafts when he saw a 3-D printer in the industrial design department and had a thought that would only occur to a longtime stop-motion aficionado with a soft spot for cool technology: This would be perfect for replacement faces.

Meanwhile, six hundred miles to the north, LAIKA was having the same epiphany; where another company might have shied away from such a radical departure from the traditional modes of animation, LAIKA saw the opportunity to elevate the craft of stop-motion. "For LAIKA," says CEO/animator Travis Knight, "Technology isn't about making the job easier or faster. Primarily it's about achieving a specific aesthetic you can't get to any other way." With this as his brief, Brian joined the LAIKA team for the film *Coraline* and dove into making this untested idea work at production scale. There were glitches and challenges, the learning-curve was steep, but the result was a level of subtlety and performance that was unlike anything before it. LAIKA never looked back.

Head of facial animation Peg Serena and lead animator Jeff Riley scour hundreds of expressions for just the right fit.

However, the first generation of 3-D printers did not print in color. That meant that for *Coraline*, each and every face needed to be hand-painted. And since the advantage of the RP approach is the ability to create an enormous range of faces, that meant a tremendous amount of painting. And that painting needed to be extremely precise. Coraline has five freckles on her right cheek, five on her left, and if they aren't always in exactly the right place then suddenly the freckles are jumping around her face in a kind of crazy way, a phenomenon the animators call *chatter*.

With *ParaNorman,* LAIKA took the process a step further, incorporating technology capable of embedding color directly on the printed faces. This new methodology baked color into the material, obviating the need to hand paint each individual face and resulting in a face with a translucent quality similar to real skin and a greater compatibility with the silicone in the puppet bodies. "That was always a problem before," said Brian. "You couldn't have a hard face next to a soft neck. With this color printer, we could put these things side by side and, apart from the seam, you can't tell the difference."

This advance meant that the revolution, begun with *Coraline*, had come to full force with *ParaNorman*. Now, not only could Brian's team print out faces with an almost unlimited range of expression, the color and texture of the skin was phenomenal.

Of course, to say the machines could print out any expression, beautifully painted, skips over a crucial step. Someone still has to tell the computer *what* to print. This is where the humans come in.

Meet Peg Serena, head of facial animation. Peg describes her job as "falling between RP and the animators" and her office is in fact located just around the corner from the RP room and right on the edge of the vast stage floor. She leads a process that is comprehensive and somewhat involved.

"The first job is to get the design of the faces right," Peg explains. She takes the character maquettes that Kent Melton and his team did and scans them to create a *turnaround*—a 360-degree image of the character head. The turnaround then goes to a 2-D artist who starts playing with that face and imagining how it moves. They work up expressions across a broad scale.

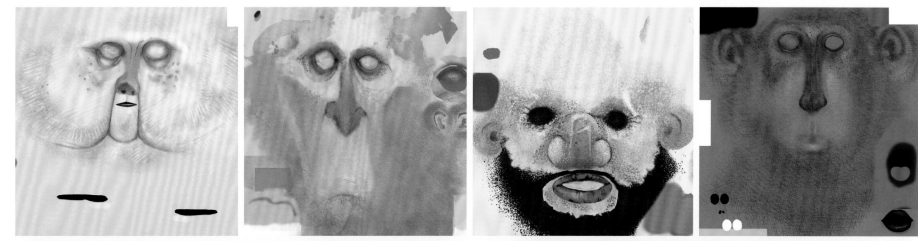

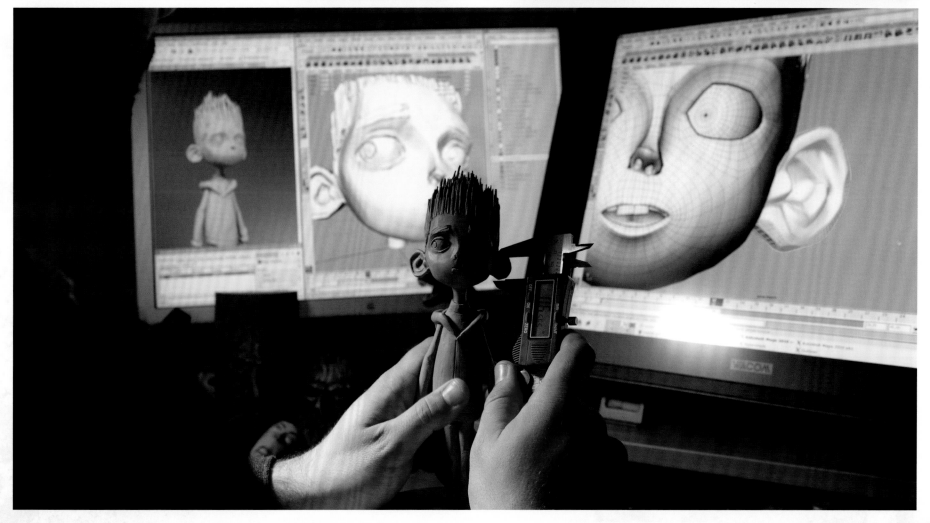

"If you shine light behind a human's ear, it glows. In live-action sometimes they'll put tape behind an actor's ear so it doesn't glow, but we embrace it. Norman's ear glows."
—BRIAN McLEAN

"We start with a neutral, relaxed face," Peg says, "then the basics: happy, mad, surprised. We do that on a scale from zero to ten—barely happy to really, really happy. Then we go overboard, really push it. Then we start doing the subtle stuff." And through it all she and the animators are working with the directors, whose feedback is precise. "The director might say, 'I don't like the way that lip curls.' They might specify the exact way they want the lip to meet the teeth, or the way the eyebrows are shaped when the character is angry. It takes a long time."

Once the broad strokes of the character are pinned down, Peg sits with the CG animators on Brian's team and they start building mouth kits—a collection of every possible mouth shape, or *phoneme*, needed to form speech or make a sound. They start with the basics but they look ahead in the script to see if there are any curveballs like screaming or demonic laughing. If it's late enough in the process that the actors have recorded their parts, Peg might even look at video of those sessions to see what kind of face an actor made when producing a certain sound.

A full range of expressions means a huge set of faces—thousands for each character—which are then printed and cataloged in the face library, a surreal depository of thousands and thousands of tiny faces neatly stored in compartmentalized plastic trays. At the same time, a digital image is taken of each face and this gets sent into editorial. When a stop-motion animator is getting ready to do a particular shot—say a piece of dialog from Blithe Hollow's resident drama teacher, tortured playwright, and ham actor, Ms. Henscher—he'll sit with a facial animation specialist who knows the library inside and out, and together they'll string together a series of faces that match the dialog and the emotion. It's called a *play-blast* and it's a powerful tool. The color is all wrong, there is no puppet body, just this face looking out from the monitor, the mouth moving, the appropriate expression flitting across the face, all synced to the recorded dialog, but it allows the animator and the directors to nail down, in advance, the exact facial performance they want. This process is repeated for every shot.

What emerges from this is a kind of shopping list—a frame-by-frame accounting of the faces the animator will need when he is on set. This goes down to the face librarians, who put together a box of faces that goes out to the set, along with an *X-sheet*—or what the Brits on the crew call a *dope sheet*—that tells the animator, among other things, which face to use for each frame. Animation Supervisor Brad Schiff says he sees the same reaction to this process every time he works with a new animator. "First they hate the idea. It's gonna rob their creativity, it takes them out of the process. Then they do it and they love it. It's liberating."

Brian McLean's theory is that the animators end up loving it because they still get to do all the facial animation, and they do it in an environment where they have total control and the opportunity to experiment without all the pressure of being on set, and with a far wider range of options than ever before. The difficult, touchy, detailed work of getting the facial expression just right can be dialed in and locked off set. Then the animator can spend his on-set time focused on getting the physical performance just right.

"RP is a game changer," McLean says proudly. Beyond the replacement faces, the art department uses it to make all sorts of custom props and the model department uses it to make spare pieces. It is an incredibly versatile, creative piece of technology to have at one's disposal. But he is quick to point out that it's just a machine, and a temperamental one at that, sensitive to changes in temperature and moisture. "The RP assistants are the unsung heroes," Brian points out. "They print the parts, sand them if needed, keep the machines running, adjust them to make up for temperature or humidity. They make the whole thing work."

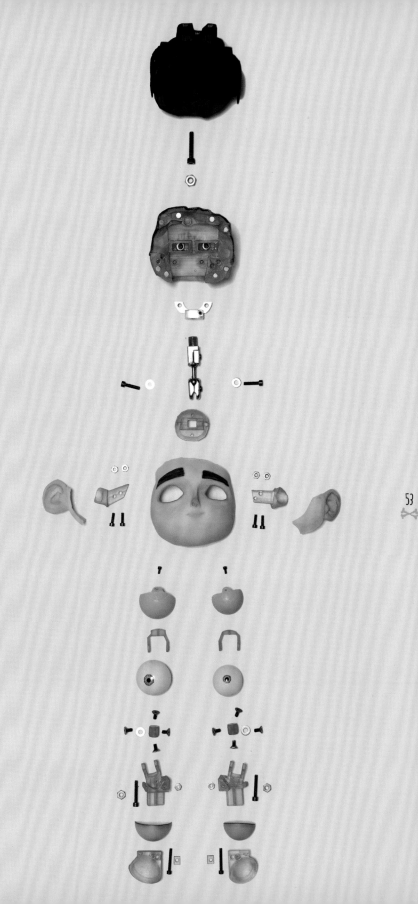

> "Everyone here loves a problem to solve, loves looking at character design and finding a way to do it. That's one of the things I love about LAIKA—it's not just, 'Oh, do it the way you did it before.' Then it becomes just a factory, churning out puppets."
> —BRIAN McLEAN

Tim Yates does a final check on a face kit before sending it off to the animator.

A plethora of printed personalities including freakishly warped faces for specific animated performances.

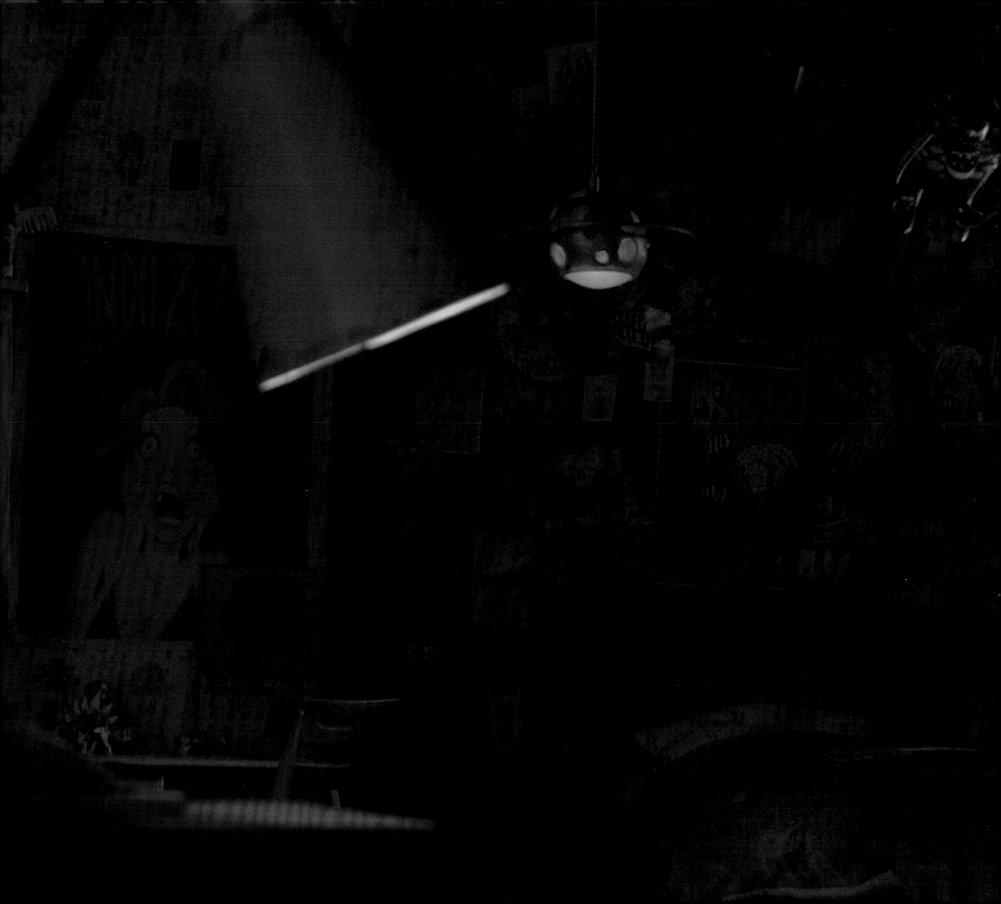

# 4

# The Workshop of Little Wonders

**Behind every great puppet**

**is an extensive team**

# THE Puppet Master

"As a kid, I didn't fit in but I really wanted to.
I always got it a little bit wrong. I made a lot of my
own clothes. As a teen I made my own wigs. I was
a hopeless student. But the doodles in the back
of my notebook, those were the best thing."
—GEORGINA HAYNS

**G**EORGINA HAYNS—but everyone calls her "George"—is officially the Creative Lead of the Puppet Department, or Puppet Head if you prefer, an enormous job that has her overseeing Kent Melton's maquette sculpting for starters, but also armature building, puppet molding, costume design, hair, and painting—all the elements, in other words, that go into making a functioning, performing puppet. And you can't have a show without a puppet—or a lot of them, really. For *ParaNorman*, when all is said and done, George and her team will have built more than two hundred individual, animatable, perfectly beautiful characters of foam and silicone and cloth and paint and metal.

She brings a rare range and depth of experience to this job, having worked for years, verging on decades, back in Britain on stop-motion shows of all types—commercials, kids' shows, features—and in a variety of roles, starting as an armaturist and moving into modeling, sculpting, costume design, and so forth.

"It was a gift to work on these shows where I got to do a little bit of everything. You can't do that on a feature," George explains. "It would be a disaster. You need people to be specialized, but I feel lucky to have had the experience to know the various jobs. It's helped me find what I think is an absolutely amazing team. And of course, I *love* people, so that helps with managing all these characters," she says, giving that distinctive North Country pronunciation to *luv*, which makes it impossible to doubt her sincerity.

During the initial sculpt, as we've seen, George hangs back a little, giving Kent the room to explore the character completely without thinking about pesky real-world problems. "I don't want Kent worrying about practical limitations. I want him to put as much emotion into the maquette as he can, and then we'll figure out how to make it move," she says. If that means he comes up with a difficult design—a character whose neck is too long or too thick to be easily animated, for example—then that is simply a challenge to the rest of the team. It's tackling these challenges, pushing the boundaries of what can be done in stop-motion, that has come to define how LAIKA approaches the art.

Once a maquette is approved, George's team meets with the directors and nails down all the performance parameters: Will it need to walk? Will it run? Jump? Climb? How realistic will its movements be? All these decisions play into what kind of armature it will have and what materials will go over this armature. In fact, it is just these sorts of decisions that are driving the conversation around the Judge's footwear. It has to look right, but it also has to be strong enough to support the puppet's weight, and to be used as a tie-down should the Judge need to be held in place during some piece of action.

Another set of decisions revolves around the character's face. Does the character need to talk—or if it's a zombie, maybe it only needs to moan? The range of expression a character needs to convey will determine how the face is animated. Will it be a mechanical face? Or will it use replacement faces cranked out through the Rapid Prototyping department?

What kind of hair will the character have? What complexion? What color eyes? Everything is a decision, every decision running through the directors and out to the teams, each decision impacting others and overlapping in complex and unexpected ways. Piece by piece the scale model is disassembled—literally pulled apart with an eye to putting it back together as a proper, working, animatable puppet.

## THE
## Skeleton Crew

ENEATH EVERY PUPPET THERE IS A KIND OF SKELETON, called the armature, and behind every armature there is an armaturist, like Jeremy Spake and his cohorts. "Each armature represents a custom solution to a particular problem." Jeremy says. "We design them in a CAD program here and then we get them milled out at a shop down the road."

Ideally, a puppet needs to be able to support its own weight—stand on its own two feet, as it were—and it would have just enough tension in the joints to hold a position, but not so much that it becomes hard for an animator to wrangle. That's doable for a character like Norman—a slim, small boy—but it becomes a challenge for the relatively immense characters like Mr. P. or Ms. Henscher, who are nearly as big as, and a bit heavier than, a newborn baby.

"We've got big puppets that are technically
challenging—characters with huge necks,
thick arms, all the no-no's in puppet making."
—CHRIS BUTLER

Just take a look at Henscher. Her arm is as big around as Norman's torso; *her* torso is shaped like a bank vault. This is an enormous puppet. And yet she is called upon to do some rather dramatic acting with sweeping hand gestures. So she is built to be strong and relatively stiff, but also mobile. And in a triumph of verisimilitude, Jeremy has built paddles into Henscher's armature so that the pendulous flesh of her upper arms—what George, being a Brit, calls her "bingo wings"—can be properly animated when she raises them to the sky.

60

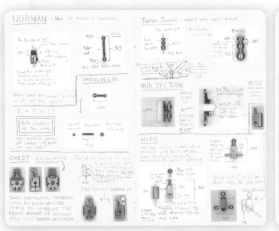
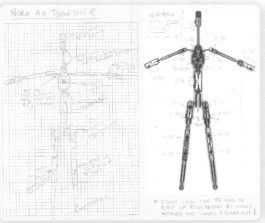
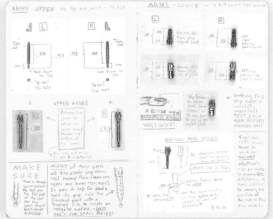

Jeremy Spake • pen

This is what an armaturist's desk/mind looks like.

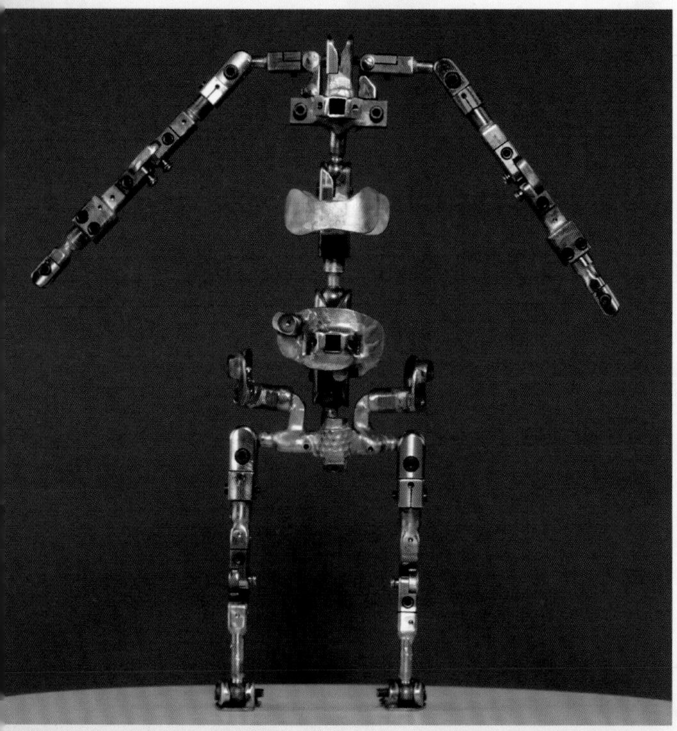

Jeremy Spake · pen

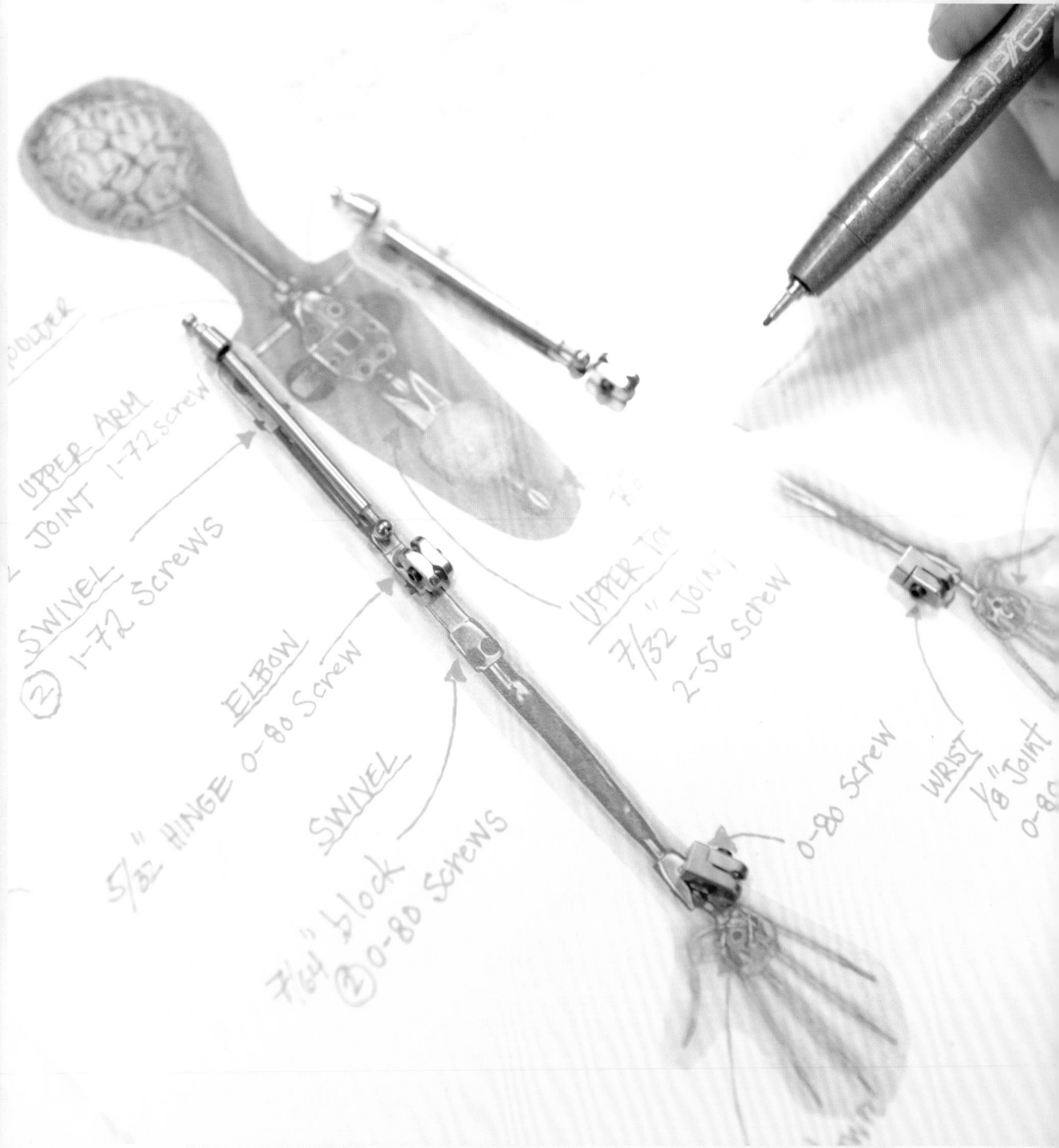

SHOULDER

UPPER ARM
JOINT 1-72 screw

SWIVEL
② 1-72 screws

ELBOW
5/32" HINGE 0-80 Screw

SWIVEL
7/64" block
② 0-80 Screws

UPPER Tri
7/32" Joint
2-56 screw

0-80 Screw

WRIST
1/8" Joint
0-80

For a cast of characters with such widely different shapes and sizes, every armature has to be custom designed and built to encompass their physical idiosyncrasies.

"The armaturist needs to be a communicator—he or she needs to know all. Where the character comes from. What the puppet will have to do. Everything."
—GEORGINA HAYNS

# CENTRAL
## Casting & Molding

THE ARMATURE FITS WITHIN A MOLD of the character—this is what gives the character its shape and bulk. "Our molders and casters are part scientist, part alchemist," says George. "They are constantly playing with the mix of materials to get a better look and better performance." For example, silicone gives a great look to a puppet, but if you cast a large puppet, like Ms. Henscher, entirely in silicone, she becomes nearly impossible for the animators to manipulate. So George's team cast Ms. Henscher in foam rubber, then cut away the surface and did a second cast of silicone to achieve a puppet that looked great and could still perform.

This was another area where early design decisions resulted in production challenges. Both Alvin and Norman's father, Perry, were designed with almost no necks—their heads just kind of merge with their shoulders. This presents a challenge for puppets that are animated using replacement faces, as typically the neck is a forgiving place to hide a seam. With Alvin and Perry, however, the tight fit of the face meant that the relatively stiff silicone skin would tend to pop the faces out during any move that involved the neck. The team responded by experimenting with adding different softeners in various amounts until they developed a recipe for a silicone that was remarkably soft yet still resisted tearing.

Where almost all of the main characters are animated using replacement faces from the RP department, there are still a few characters with mechanical heads—notably the zombies—and these too fall under George's realm. Beneath the silicone skin, a mechanical head reminds one of the best

> "I still can't believe this is happening. There have been days I've seen armies of people slaving over the tiniest bits of detail, and I think, 'Oh god, what have I done to them?'"
> —CHRIS BUTLER

Swiss watchmaking—it is a tiny marvel of gears and joints, and allows the animator to move the face through a range of expressions. A turn of this screw drops the jaw. This screw activates gears that raise the lips in a sneer. A mechanical head doesn't allow for the same subtlety of expression you can get from a replacement face—but zombies aren't known for their subtlety. For a zombie, it is important that the jaws be able to drop and swing, as though the face were almost coming apart, as long-dead zombies tend to do. Mechanical heads deliver this beautifully.

And the faces aren't the only parts of the zombies that seem in danger of dropping off. In fact at one crucial moment in the film, a zombie actually loses a hand which then skitters about with a life of its own. The model makers simply built a stunt zombie with a detachable hand for this particular scene so that the animator could remove it at will.

Of course, the modelers will point out that animators are constantly removing hands by mistake—these tiny, fragile limbs are also natural grab points and, throughout filming, they are forever bending and breaking. So George's team makes extras—every main character will have multiple sets of spare hands, modeled ahead of time and carefully, painstakingly painted to match.

A squelchy silicone brain is manufactured ready to be impaled by a puppet's stiletto heel.

The vibrant puppet workshop in which armaturists, painters, mold makers, and wig makers work shoulder to shoulder.

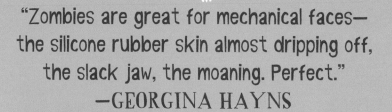

66

Puppets and maquettes in various stages of completion clutter every available surface in the puppet department.

A character's body parts are molded individually before being assembled into a functioning puppet.

## Puppet Painting

**E**VERYBODY KNOWS what it means to say, "so-and-so has a twinkle in her eye." It's that ineffable spark of life that somehow lights up a face. But in stop-motion, that twinkle can't be ineffable. It has to be painted, over and over.

Amy Wulfing is the head of puppet painting. She and her six-person team are the people responsible for creating that twinkle, or that scowl, or that ghoulish pallor, or, for that matter, the particular rotten-but-not-disgusting quality of the zombies' flesh. All these things, working through the director, are painted onto the models, again and again, by hand, by Amy's team.

Take Norman's eyes as an example. As the lead character, Norman was one of the first to be tackled, so he was a proving ground for a lot of decisions. The directors knew he would have striking blue eyes and they knew that they should be somewhat asymmetrical and outsized, rather than strictly realistic. Amy's team went to work, starting with paint on paper, putting as many as a dozen eye options in front of the directors. From this they narrowed the range. The team explored and refined. The directors narrowed it further. They tried these refinements on actual eyes—actual puppet eyes—which they fitted in a model, placed on a properly lit set, and photographed. In the end, Norman's eye is a composition of six different colors of paint, painstakingly applied to a sphere less than a quarter inch across.

That's the eyes. Take this attention to detail and craft and apply it now to the faces, the hands, the mouths of a couple dozen characters, all of which exist in multiple copies, and you begin to get a sense of the scale of work.

Color RP has lightened the painter's load somewhat. On *Coraline*, where LAIKA first pioneered the use of Rapid Prototyping to print out puppet faces, the machines did not print in color, which meant that each of the hundreds if not thousands of different facial expressions for each character would have to be painted by hand. The work was enormous.

On *ParaNorman*, LAIKA began pioneering the use of color RP. "With this process," Amy said, "we didn't have to limit ourselves to what was repeatable by hand. We could do anything the directors could possibly dream of." The painters still paint the characters' expressions but these expressions are then made into a digital file, manipulated, and printed out, precisely, again and again. This opened up creative avenues and saved a tremendous amount of labor, but it did create a new job in the process. Someone now needed to transfer the painter's art, right down to the texture of the brush or pencil strokes, into a computer file. Happily, one of Amy's painters, Tory Bryant, was also adept at computer graphics. "Having someone who understood the painter's process and could translate that to the computer—that was awesome for us," Amy explained.

The painters are also called on to put the finishing touches on a character's wardrobe—splotches of dirt, signs of wear or age. It can be daunting, Amy says. "Here you have this beautiful, one-of-a-kind creation and you are about to apply paint to it—you don't get a second shot. There's not another copy of this. It represents hours and hours—maybe hundreds of hours, of someone's life."

Josh Storey applies the finishing touches to a zombie's silicone skin.

"Norman is a perfect puppet. One of the best I've ever worked with. Because everything needs to be so lifelike and subtle, you need to not be fighting with the puppet."
—DAN ALDERSON, animator

## Clothes

### MAKE THE PUPPET

BEFORE THE HANDS WERE PAINTED, before the first mold was cast, before any armatures were made, back when there was just Chris Butler's script and some early sketches, Deborah Cook, *ParaNorman*'s head costume designer, was already digging into the project. For her, it starts with research, and what better place to research the attitude and attire of New England's founding Puritans than back in olde England, Deb's home. She made her own pilgrimage to libraries and archives in the towns from which New England's settlers embarked some three hundred years ago and began looking into what people were saying, thinking, and wearing. She began collecting scraps and photos and sketches that reflected what was on her mind and bit by bit a picture of these people came together. Our image of Puritan New England is typically restrained and dour, but Cook also saw a resourceful, ingenious people, pioneers, whose clothing had surprising embellishments—stitching, buckled shoes, wide belts, and capes. "Who wears capes anymore?" Cook exclaimed.

Meanwhile, there was a second period of New England life, the modern day, to be explored and developed. Again, for Cook, wardrobe is an opportunity to help tell the story—what are the socioeconomics, what is the mood, what cultural references hold sway? Writer/director Butler was influenced by childhood favorite *Scooby Doo*, and Cook clearly picked up on that. When the protagonists stand side by side on the courthouse steps, we see bits of Velma, Fred, Shaggy, and Daphne, but not where you expect them to be. They are mixed up and reimagined for this new world.

A big challenge for wardrobe in stop-motion is finding materials that are fine enough to read at this scale, yet still have enough substance to perform. Cook has a library of materials and goes on shopping missions to stock up for a show, but she still keeps her eyes open when she is out and about, always hoping for that surprise discovery.

There is a technical aspect to costume that isn't readily visible on the surface. Cook and her team work with the puppet makers and armaturists to determine where the clothing will attach to the puppet to ensure that it moves and flows along with the character, rather than simply hanging there, stiff as a board. Sometimes an armature or bit of wire will be built into a piece of clothing to let the animator give it some performance. An outsized example of this is the Judge's cloak, which would appear to be a simple piece of cloth but in fact needs to be able to be formed and moved so that it seems to flap in the wind, one frame at a time.

When the animation process gets rolling, there will be twenty or more animators each working on a different shot, so a main character—like Norman or Courtney or Neil—might be on a number of sets simultaneously. Hence the need for multiple character puppets. For the costume department, this means that every "one-of-a-kind" outfit needs to be precisely duplicated several times. Cook has a protocol in place that involves detailed documentation of steps, including high-res photos and stitch counts, so that every Norman costume looks exactly the same.

Even after every costume is made, the costume department is kept busy, repairing damaged clothes or running onto set and opening a seam to let an armaturist get at the joints with an Allen wrench to adjust the tension when necessary, then sewing it back up again when he or she is done. It's difficult, exacting work, but the reward comes when the end result is up there on the big screen, magnified for the world to see.

---

"The clothing needs armatures as well; it needs to move frame by frame, if it's going to move at all. Sometimes the Judge's cloak flies behind him—he has special action cloaks for the big scenes."
—GEORGINA HAYNS

70

Costume designer Deborah Cook relishing the minutiae of her daily toil.

Heidi Smith • pencil

Heidi Smith • pencil

Scarf:
Sits between hoodie
and hairline
angled straight
edges.

Red Thread through
it & a lighter
brown than the scarf
itself.

NIKESPORTSWEAR

73

74

Heidi Smith • pencil

Custom made fabric prints share the same skewed lines and asymmetry as the characters who will wear them.

Ross Stewart • digital

# WHO DOES YOUR
## Hair

**L**AST, BUT CERTAINLY NOT LEAST, comes the hair. Here, as everywhere in stop-motion, there is a surprising amount of complexity underlying something we all take for granted. For Jill Penny, *ParaNorman*'s hair and fur lead, that complexity is the challenge she happily grapples with throughout the day and, sometimes, even in her dreams.

"In stop-motion, straight hair past the shoulders is the biggest nightmare in the whole entire world," Jill explains. "It has to interact with the shoulders as the puppet moves, and the straightness of it, the physics of it, makes it challenging to tension the hair so that it can move naturally without strange buckles." Courtney, Norman's sister, has long, relatively straight hair, relieved by a saucy curl of a pony tail well below her shoulders. What's more, her hair is blond. Blond hair is almost transparent, so it is much more difficult to hide the wires that give the hair its structure. And, as Jill quickly discovered, the traditional adhesives used to affix the hair to the wires retain their flexibility, which is great, but also their tackiness, which is not so great for blond hair. "Within literally seconds of being on set, you could see the dust and grime collecting on the hair."

The hair team, led by Head of Department Jessica Lynn, fashioned a unique "do" for every character in the movie.

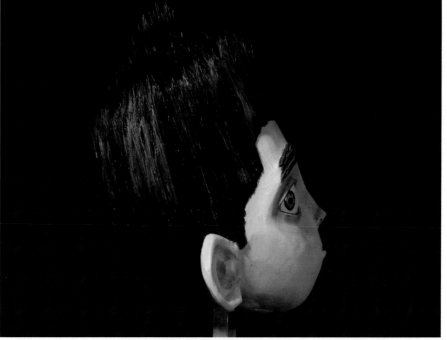

"You often find that people who get into stop-motion animation aren't trained in animation—they are natural born craftspeople who want to work on a small scale, who are incredibly patient."
—GEORGINA HAYNS

Various materials and treatments were explored to find the right kind of curl for Neil's signature frizzy hair.

The solution to that problem came in a straightforward fashion. Jill did some experimentation and came up with a new adhesive that wouldn't stay sticky but would stay flexible. But the tricky problem of how to animate straight hair still remained. She pondered it and pondered it and then, one morning, awoke with the answer straight from a dream. She rushed into work and tried it out—rather than gluing the hair to the wires, she encased each wire in a sheath and then glued the hair to that. The wire was free to rotate and slide inside the sheath, but still gave support to the hair.

To her delight it worked for Courtney, whose long blond ponytail needed to have a life of its own. Courtney's mom, Sandra, with her big bobbed hairdo, received the Courtney treatment times seven—seven separate segments of sheathed wires and hair joined together in one formidable do. And finally, this new invention of Jill's met perhaps the toughest challenge, Norman's friend Salma, with her perfectly straight tresses.

These were the most technical challenges Jill and the hair department faced, but the thing she loves about her job is how every character is a new puzzle to solve. Mr. Prenderghast had a beard so large that it extended below the face seam and was actually part of the body mold. "I had to find a way to make the two parts of the beard meld," Jill said. "So I did a test beard and discovered you could make it from foam latex. Then I just let the mold guys deal with it. Problem solved."

> ## "With the dead guys, we're always trying to make them a little fun too."
> ### —SAM FELL

For the zombies, the directors wanted a more crinkly, papery hairstyle. Jill took the challenge head on: "There was this drawer of materials we weren't using—nonsynthetic things. I had to figure out what kind of adhesives would work with these more natural materials and then I just started trying things out until I got something really gnarly."

The job also entails turf battles with other departments over the limited space on the head. When the RP guys want to put a big screw in the middle of the wig cap, Jill finds herself negotiating for the space to get her gear in. They say they want the space, she says she needs the space, and somehow it all works out. And then there are the inevitable on-set hair emergencies, where she or a team member will need to whisk in to repair or replace a damaged coif.

It's unusual work, detailed and demanding work, and it takes a lot out of Jill. But, like so many of the people in this big, scattered warren of workshops and sets, she feels like this work is what she was meant to do. Yes, it's just doll hair, but Jill is determined that it will be the best doll hair ever. This attitude is pervasive in LAIKA; the place runs on a personal dedication to craft multiplied hundreds of times over.

81

O N A STOP-MOTION FILM, the art department is responsible for the overall look of the film, which is a kind of high-level way of saying they make all the *stuff*—the sets, the buildings, the lampposts, the grass, the trees, the cars, the sky, the sun if you see the sun, the moon if there is a moon, the fire hydrants on the street, the gas meters on the house, the neon sign above the bar, the cracks in the pavement—basically anything you see that isn't a character. It's a huge job, so it's a huge department, with many subdepartments—a painting department, a modeling department, set construction, greens—and in charge of it all, one cool customer named Nelson Lowry.

Lowry, youthful, fit, tattooed, is nevertheless a veteran in this business. In fact saying he's a vet is like saying John Wayne has done a few Westerns. Lowry began his career sweeping up at a studio in New York and has learned mold making, puppet making, set dressing, you name it, working his way up to production lead on some of the biggest stop-motion films of the last ten years. He has seen it all and done it all and you get the sense that he is that unflappable guy a director could lean on in times of trouble.

First thing to know about art directing a feature-length stop-motion film: "Everything starts with the characters," Lowry states. "The environments are born from the characters. They exist to support the characters and the story." Norman, of course, is our main character and his environment is Blithe Hollow, a particular kind of New England town with a lot of past and not so much present—it's a little down-at-the-heels and prone to bask overly in its colonial history. As it happens, Lowry grew up in New England, in Massachusetts specifically, in a mill town that had seen better days, so he connected immediately with the script.

83

One of the first things Lowry did when he came on board the project was to join the directors on a road trip back to the New England he knew. They got a location scout and went to see the real-world analog of every place they could think of from the script. They went to Salem, of course, with its witch-tourist kitsch, but more importantly they visited some of the scrappy towns that are a little less preserved in amber—Braintree, Brockton, Weymouth. Here they got the feel for the neighborhoods, the schools, that patch of pine woods between the schoolyard and the river. They saw the houses and soaked up the detail. Director Sam Fell, whose sense of boundaries may be less developed than others', was shouted out of more than one backyard. But even this experience gave them a taste of the tension running just beneath the surface in these towns, a tension you can feel running through the adults in *ParaNorman*—in Norman's dad Perry, in Ms. Henscher, even, in its ancestral form, in the Judge.

The color of the film is a kind of glue that holds the work together, gives it a consistent feel, an identifiable "look." Lowry tends to like to keep color to a limited palette so that the film isn't "all over the place," in his words. "The color has to be incredibly cohesive. So I try to pare down the amount of color in the film so you can be specific about it. I tried to make it feel like New England, down to the color of the cars in the street, the color of the houses." One detail that came out of Lowry's childhood in Massachusetts: "Sometimes, maybe a paint place was going out of business, so they'd be selling off the stock that's left. And you'll go through a neighborhood and see all these

houses painted the same color. That kind of detail—it doesn't have to be overt, the audience doesn't even have to notice—but it adds to a sense of reality, it makes it feel like a real place, that's important in animation. You can be so fanciful and arbitrary in animation that it's nice when you ground it in the real thing."

Now Blithe Hollow had a look, but it still needed a map. Lowry sat down with an environment designer, literally sat down on the floor of the production area, and started laying out blocks—this one is Norman's house, here's the school, here's the graveyard. They started with Google Maps printouts of small New England towns, just to get the layout. Then they simplified and narrowed until they had something the directors loved. They transferred it to a computer model, tinkered with it some more, and finally built a tabletop model of the whole town.

It's extensive work, but for Lowry it was just another way that good art direction serves the story. There's a lot of running around in *ParaNorman*: they're at the school, at the graveyard, in town, back to the graveyard. "Having that figured out, so that the steeple you see over Norman's shoulder in one

> "Sam Fell tromped through the woods and found the perfect backyard, which we photographed and built lovingly by hand."
> —NELSON LOWRY

scene is in the right place three scenes later, that just gives you a sense that this is a real place," Lowry says.

There is the planning part of the job, which is considerable, and then there is the building part, which is enormous and has to happen fast. Take a character like Mr. P. The team has to quickly imagine, "Who is this man? What is he like? What's in his closet?" and then all the items that fill out the story have to be built by hand.

"We make trips to the hardware store, to the craft store, machine stuff on our lathes, but sometimes design comes out of necessity," Lowry says. He describes prowling through the LAIKA building, looking in corners, diving in dumpsters, looking for some piece of scrap that will inspire something. By the time they're done, Mr. P.'s house is almost bursting with books and photos and tchotchkes, the by-product of his eclectic, eccentric life. And every one of those items—from the taxidermied velociraptor head, to the net filled with forks and knives hanging from the ceiling, to the dreamcatchers—means something to one of the crew members.

Nature is notoriously hard to capture in stop-motion—the rich detail, the fractal patterns, the lack of any straight lines—and in keeping with the LAIKA tradition of not shying away from challenges, *ParaNorman* contains a lot of nature scenes. And here, the inventive, problem-solving side of the art department is on full display. The maquettes for the forest—trees made from corrugated cardboard wrapped around PVC pipe and thrown together in a couple of hours—were meant to be placeholders, just something to think about until the real things could be made. But once they were built they had a kind of organic texture that felt surprisingly real. So they went into the movie.

Ross Stewart • pen (top), digital (bottom)

> "I think the thing that we've really been striving for on this movie is the *ParaNorman* effect: Trying to keep positive information in blank spaces. Same with texture and paint. You don't create uniformity and patterns on everything. It guides your eye, so you're not bombarded with detail and information."
> —ALICE BIRD, assistant art director

Pete Oswald · digital

Some solutions are high-tech: bits of doll-sized hardware printed on the Rapid Prototype machine or cast from elaborate molds. Others are refreshingly low-tech: The ground cover is just shredded paper towels. The leaves are made from craft paper Lowry found in a recycling bin, which he treated with a wetting agent to get the right translucent look of a leaf just losing its green and starting to turn.

In one scene Norman walks across a landscape of cracked earth, but it proved hard to paint a crack pattern that felt authentic. Someone had the idea to drop a bowling ball on a sheet of plate glass. The glass was procured, somebody else came up with a bowling ball, and after a satisfying bit of trial and error, a convincing crack pattern was produced. It's a detail, but it's a detail you can feel, and these details run through the fabric of the entire project.

The directors wanted a naturalistic, almost live-action feel to the town, but being true to the setting does not mean being a slave to reality. Take a walk down the main street of Blithe Hollow to see this point in practice. From the dry cleaner to the tavern to the electronics shop with its TVs playing in the window, to the supermarket with its spectral neon glow, this is the prototypical working-class town, very true to form. But look closely and you'll see that not a single window is a real rectangle; there is no roofline that doesn't swoop or jag. "If one of our characters were to walk into a room and sit next to you, you'd find his proportions grotesque," Lowry points out. "The huge head, the hands out of proportion, too much neck or no neck at all. They aren't real in

their form. And we have to build rooms where they feel comfortable, like they belong. So the rooms are a little skewed, a little off-kilter. The set shop just loves getting these drawings with no straight lines anywhere—but that's what it takes."

Like so many people you meet at LAIKA, Lowry genuinely loves his work and seems perfectly suited to it. "It's great fun," he says, "but it is a long slog. We've got such a strong team here, picked from all over the world, with so much experience from all different disciplines. We've pushed the medium—from the RP propping to the rigging to the costumes to the puppets; the sets and stylization are so thorough that it really feels new, it's not referencing anything else, it feels like its own world. And I think each of us, from the leads to the crew, feels like we're part of something special.

When you watch *ParaNorman*, Nelson Lowry doesn't want you to notice the art direction. He wants you to feel it. And if, on the second or third viewing, you start to observe the care, the artistry, the obsessive attention to detail, he wants you to know it was the end result of a concerted effort by a truly remarkable team. "To see this team present stuff to me, and think, 'OK, that's better than I would've asked for' . . . how often does that happen? Well, with these guys, it happens all the time."

Early Ross Stewart pencil sketches were realized three dimensionally by production designer Nelson Lowry.

"I love the look of this movie. It is so freaking well observed. It has charm, and grace, but it's not afraid to applaud ugly."
—CHRIS BUTLER

Every location in the movie can be traced back to something tangibly real, thanks to early research trips to Massachusetts.

92

Ross Stewart • digital

Ross Stewart • digital

"You borrow things from your life, from
people you've met—I've got a catalog in my head
of stuff I'm waiting to use."
—NELSON LOWRY

Ross Stewart • digital

94
⚔

Ross Stewart and Trevor Dalmer • digital and digital paint

Pete Oswald and Trevor Dalmer • digital and digital paint

"Originally the story was set around Halloween, but we brought it back to early fall. I was excited about the way the green drains out of the trees just before they turn orange and red, so our green is not super vibrant; it's a late summer green with splashes of color as the leaves start to turn."

—NELSON LOWRY

Pete Oswald * digital

Pete Oswald and Trevor Dalmer * digital and digital paint

Ross Stewart and Trevor Dalmer · digital and digital paint

Pete Oswald · digital

"The time of day was something we plotted very carefully. Innately, your mind kind of knows tonally where you are in terms of where the sun is, as you go through the pale gold and the pinks and apricots down to that deep salmon red just before the sun goes down behind that mountain. And similarly, your shadows go from a neutral gray, through to a strange lilac hue, and then down to a black. Humans have a clock that works off that spectrum."
—TRISTAN OLIVER, director of photography

Ross Stewart • digital

Ross Stewart • pen and ink

Pete Oswald and Trevor Dalmer • digital and digital paint

Ross Stewart • digital

BLITHE MIDDLE SCHOOL

B M S

BLITHE MIDDLE SCHOOL

JULY 6 CANTEEN FIRE
 8 SIX, DRUGS,
 ROCK AND ROLL
 9 FIGHT CLUB

Ross Stewart • pen and ink

Ross Stewart and Trevor Dalmer • digital and digital paint

102

Ross Stewart • digital

Ean McNamara • digital

Pete Oswald • digital

Ross Stewart and Trevor Dalmer • digital and digital paint

Ross Stewart and Trevor Dalmer • digital and digital paint

Ross Stewart • digital

Ross Stewart • pen and ink

Ean McNamara • digital

Pete Oswald • digital

"It's always a great feeling when you've delivered a set, the dresser has done their thing, and you just step back and it's exactly like the concept art. You just want to step into that scene. You know exactly what that environment feels like. The school—you can smell the sweaty kids. You know you've done your job."
—ALICE BIRD

Ross Stewart and Ean McNamara • digital

Pete Oswald · digital

Chris Turnham • digital

Ross Stewart • digital

Pete Oswald • digital

Dave Vandervoort • digital

Ean McNamara • digital

Ross Stewart  digital

Alan Cook  digital

Ross Stewart and Trevor Dalmer  digital and digital paint

Trevor Dalmer • digital

Ross Stewart • pen and ink

Ross Stewart • pen and ink

Ross Stewart • digital

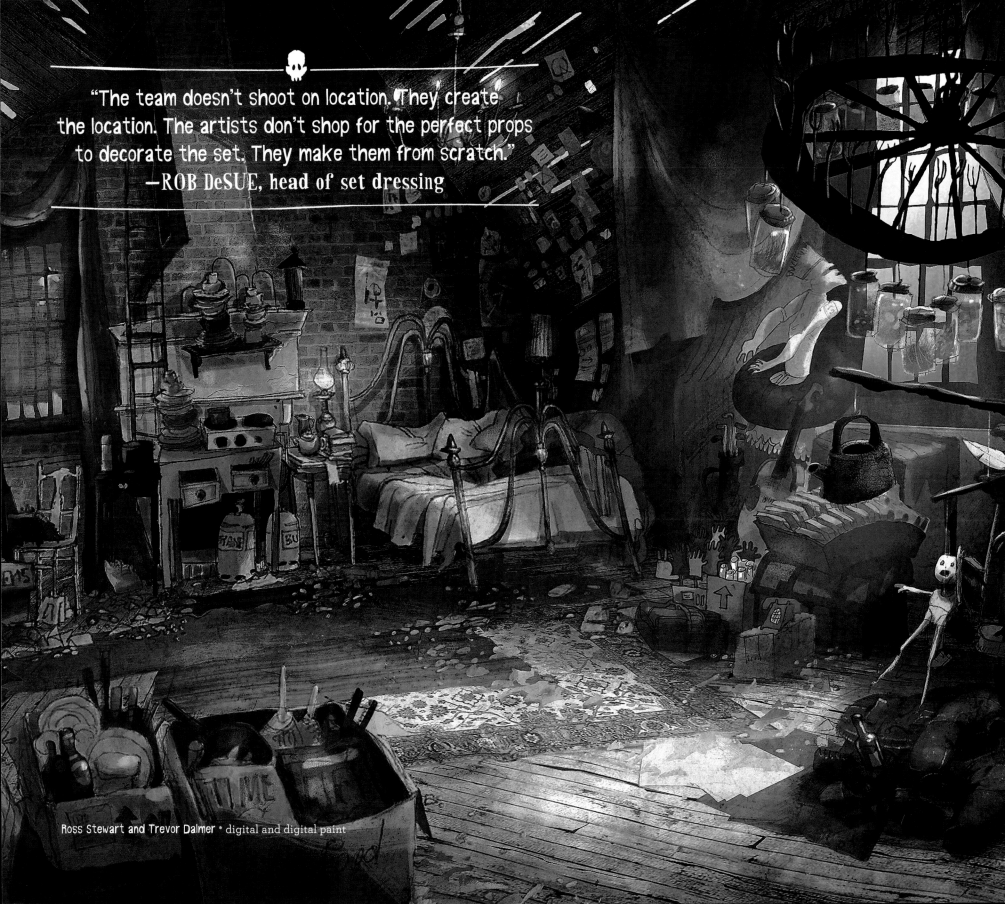

"The team doesn't shoot on location. They create the location. The artists don't shop for the perfect props to decorate the set. They make them from scratch."
—ROB DeSUE, head of set dressing

Ross Stewart and Trevor Dalmer • digital and digital paint

Ross Stewart • digital

Pete Oswald • digital

Ross Stewart • digital

"The sinking, sagging New England houses, we just took further. A lot came out of Ross Stewart's rough illustrations and before they could clean them up, I'd take them and say, 'No, no, this is beautiful.'"
—NELSON LOWRY

Ross Stewart • pen and ink

Ean McNamara • digital

Nelson Lowry • digital

Pete Oswald • digital

Pete Oswald • digital

Heidi Smith * pencil

Ross Stewart * pen and ink

116

Heidi Smith * pencil

Ean McNamara * digital

Pete Oswald • digital

# Where the Story Comes to Life

## The men and women behind the curtains

**W**E BEGAN WITH THE SPARK OF AN IDEA in Chris Butler's brain, moved out through Heidi Smith's tiny workspace into the quiet hum of the story department, then the bustle and buzz of the puppet department, out into the workshops of the art department, and each step of the way the scale and energy grew. Now we have arrived on the stage floor, which dwarfs everything that came before. The scale of it is humbling, and the feeling of it—the black curtains hanging floor to ceiling in long, somber rows—is almost sacred, yet a visitor can't help feeling a little giddy. This is the chocolate factory, this is Wonderland, this is Narnia. Behind those curtains is mystery and magic. It makes you feel like a kid just to be near it.

There are fifty shooting units of various size on the LAIKA stage floor, all cordoned off behind drapes hung from scaffolding. Here is the main street of Blithe Hollow, over there is the courthouse, down the row is Norman's house, followed by a small unit in which is re-created in loving, grungy detail the boys' lavatory at Norman's school. The set is trundled in here and unpacked and then the set dressers go to work adding all the details—the dirt, the rust, what the director of photography (DP), Tristan Oliver, rather poetically describes as the *patina*-tion of real life. "When the set goes in," he says, "it is perfect but dead. The set dressers make it start to breathe."

119

That deep respect for the art direction is an ingrained part of Oliver's craft. He got his start in the early days of Aardman Animation, when that studio was igniting a kind of renaissance of stop-motion filmmaking with films like *Wrong Trousers* and *A Grand Day Out*. He learned early on that the art department was the partner of the camera department and that a good working relationship led to better results. "Someone told me early on, 'They build what we shoot.'" In other words, there is a kind of symbiosis wherein, in order for the art direction to shine, the sets must be beautifully shot, and in order for the photography to shine, the camera must be pointed at beautiful sets.

Much of Oliver's art comes down to lighting—how do you take a set built on a small scale and light it to feel as natural and believable as a live-action production? "The old-school animation approach of just putting up flat lights so there were no shadows—we've moved right away from that. We're not afraid to let the highlights burn out; we're not afraid to let the shadows go to black." The first thing Oliver did when coming on to *ParaNorman*, months before shooting began, was to pull together a reel of references—films and stills that captured the feeling he wanted from the filmography. Says Oliver, "My main sources for the look were the movies *Atonement* and *Road to Perdition*, as well as *House of Flying Daggers*, *Hero*, and *Crouching Tiger, Hidden Dragon*, all of which use color in a very interesting way. For the ghost look, I was referencing early color system stills, in particular the Lumière brothers' Autochrome pictures and the works of the Russian Prokudin-Gorskii, which gave us the idea for breaking the edges of the ghosts into color layers."

Oliver shared this with directors Fell and Butler and with Nelson Lowry, the head of the art department. Together they agreed on a kind of style bible that included a color palette, ideas about how different times of day were to be represented, a point of view on how the 3-D effect was to be employed, and so on. "Before we ever shot a frame," Oliver said, "I had something to share with my crew so we were all coming from the same place."

That shared vision is crucial in a project with fifty shooting units and twenty-two animators but a camera crew of just twenty across all the roles—lead cameras, camera assistants, motion control operators, electricians. Oliver puts it this way: "The camera crew is like a herd of wildebeest in a way. We go

"It has to be a collaboration (with the art department). I'm allowed to go in there and say, "I think this color is a bit wrong" and they can come to me and say, "I think this lighting is a bit wrong," and there is absolutely no problem. That's how it should work."
—TRISTAN OLIVER

into the set, get it ready, and at the moment it's ready to shoot, we move on to the next set." Everyone has to be on the same page—"shooting the house style," as Oliver says—to ensure consistency in the final film.

Lighting a relatively small set can require some surprisingly big lights, particularly for a scene like Norman's arrival at school. "People always think, well, the sets are tiny, so we must use tiny lights and, of course, we do use a number of small lighting fixtures, but we also use some very big lights because when you are lighting a big exterior, daytime, you want it to look like the sun is shining. If you have a small light, you find the shadows are all skewing outward and you can tell, very obviously, the light source is a small luminette. What you want is a big light, so the shadows feel natural. And we've got some very, very big lights."

On the other hand, some scenes call for an entirely different approach. "Main Street at night has a very real look," says Oliver. "Every shop has a different colored light. On a street you'll have a bar with a neon sign, you'll have a launderette with white fluorescents coming out of it, you'll have sodium street lights. Our aim was to make it super-colored and then add just a little bit more so that when the zombies come into that environment, they look great. All that colored light onto that green flesh works very nicely." To achieve that look, Oliver relies on miniature-lighting specialist Matt DeLau. "Any light that's in front of the camera," DeLau says, "that's me." For Main Street that means miniature street lights, miniature neon signs, miniature fluorescent lights—even the eight miniature TVs in the window at Blithe Hollow TV World.

But in the end, it isn't the difficult bits you remember—if they're done well enough, you may not even notice them. In the end, it's a question of believing in and connecting with the characters on the screen. As DP Tristan Oliver puts it: "I think, inevitably, it's the simple stuff you feel the best about. There is a lot of tricky stuff in this film—zombies and ghosts and so forth—but I think if you can get a good-looking daylight exterior and nail it, *that's* an achievement. There's one shot in the film—it's a sunny day, the turmoil has subsided, they're in a field and you can hear the birds chirping and the sun is streaming down—that, I think, is the best-looking shot in the movie. We've nailed it. The set's right, the lighting is right, the choice of lens is right, and it doesn't need anything doing. And when we showed it to the directors the first time, they said, 'We haven't got anything to add.' That for me is as good as it gets."

Finally, before the set can be turned over to the animators, the riggers have to do their work. "Our department defies gravity," says rigging supervisor Ollie Jones. "We are responsible for any time the puppet is in the air—whether it's running or jumping or falling. We build and design the structure that supports it, frame by frame." In *ParaNorman* the riggers faced the extra challenge presented by the ghostly characters who never touch down. "We used a gimbal and extra pivots," Jones says, "to make sure they could move with a kind of ghostly feel."

Typically the riggers meet with the animators to go over what kind of motion the scene will require. Then they go to work on the set for a half-day or more before turning it over to the animators. Like ninjas of the animation world, if the riggers have done their job right, you will never even know they were there. Their work—as detailed and exacting as it is—is designed to disappear.

---

"When you see these characters on screen, they aren't puppets. They are alive. My job is to make that happen."
—JUSTIN RASCH

Alan Cook · pen and ink

Up to now, everything has been a team effort. We've seen the story process, character design, puppet fabrication, the RP process, art direction, and set building—intense, iterative work involving teams of people with the direct and continuous oversight of the directors. But a single frame has yet to be shot.

And we are almost there. But before the animator goes up on his shot, he or she will sit down with the directors and talk through a plan for the action. The next step is to block the shot—the animator takes the puppets and moves them through the key poses. For a ten-second piece that might be five poses; the animator exposes five frames. This goes back to the editor, who cuts it together with the correct timing. The directors and the animator then look at this rough sequence and adjust as necessary. Then it's on to rehearsal, which is essentially a run-through of the full performance but filmed on 2s or 3s or 4s, which is to say, every 2nd, 3rd, or 4th frame, depending on the complexity of the shot. Then this goes back into editorial for one more look with the directors. It's a time-consuming process, of course, but it ensures that there are no nasty surprises in the final performance.

Now that the lighting is perfected and the set dressed, the riggers are satisfied and have moved on. The animator closes the curtain behind him and he is alone. And the animation—in the truly old-school sense of the word, meaning "to bring life"—begins.

"Stop-motion puppets are like little vampires, feeding off the vitality of the people that handle them. Every bit of life you see onscreen is life that's been sucked out of an animator."
—TRAVIS KNIGHT, CEO/animator

To make the inanimate move, seemingly of its own free will, is one thing, but to make it act, to really get up and *dance*, is something else entirely. Stop-frame animation has, by its practical nature, always skirted the periphery of naturalism. It has been far more concerned as a medium with the macabre or the theatrical or the surreal. While the Nine Old Men of the Walt Disney Studio were perfecting the clean lines and bright colors of their own brand of illusory life, stop-motion was playing with dead things in the shadows. There has always been considerable charm to the raw romance of the puppet pushing process, and LAIKA celebrates this great tradition still, but on *ParaNorman* the studio wanted to shift its perspective a little.

In *ParaNorman*, the style of animation in itself is one of the movie's biggest challenges. The movie aspires to go beyond the kind of acting we've seen before in stop-motion. In keeping with the creators' take on the naturalistic (as oppose to realistic) look of its world and characters, the animation here is all about true observation. This isn't a cartoon. It is neither whimsy nor magic. It has weight and scale and subtlety and restraint. This is as real as acting gets. In this practical medium where the kind of total control that one can achieve in a wholly digital world is almost an impossibility, this is a bold ambition indeed. It is an endeavor as inspired by the technical innovations that raise the game in the other departments all around the studio, as it is by the cinematic nature of the story itself.

Clearly, it isn't easy.

It is exacting work, detailed and exhausting both mentally and physically. The stage floors are concrete and the animator is on his feet ten to twelve hours a day. The sets are built for puppets, not for people, and an animator needs to be part acrobat, part contortionist to get in and around these miniature worlds. Animator Justin Rausch worked as a stuntman in Hollywood for years before serendipity turned his hobby into his profession: He calls animation "the most mentally demanding and physically draining work I have ever done." As Travis Knight points out, "You're responsible for tracking potentially dozens of elements, some as small as a grain of sand, and they each need to move in a particular way. You have to be totally focused for long stretches of time."

122

Nelson Lowry • collage

"In stop-motion, nothing moves of its own volition. Everything you see is evidence of a human hand and a human mind. Every physical detail, every blade of grass, every branch of every tree, every emotion on every character's face was designed, built, and manipulated by an artist's hand."
—TRAVIS KNIGHT

Ean McNamara • digital

Set dresser Duncan Gillis grapples with faux foliage.

"We used to joke, "Is Payton still in the bathroom? . . .
Yeah, he's still in there." That was a complicated sequence."
—BRAD SCHIFF

Animation Supervisor Brad Schiff would back him up on that. "It's hard, sometimes lonely work," he says. "You see animators, when they're in the middle of it, walking around with that thousand-yard stare. I joke that every time I do a job my social skills diminish a little more."

It is almost impossible to overstate the amount of care and time and attention that goes into the shooting process. An animator lives with a sequence for weeks, if not months, and for some of the complicated shots it can be still longer. For example, the sequence in the lavatory of Norman's school, which involves a ghost emerging from a toilet and some very ghostly swirling toilet paper, occupied just about a year of animator Payton Curtis's life.

Of course, *ParaNorman* is full of challenging sequences. The long, dramatic chase scene involving the Judge and the van feels more *Bullitt* than stop-motion. Coby Lorang, the model maker who specializes in vehicles (*ParaNorman*'s resident "car guy"), says the sequence kept him hopping with van repairs. "The Judge was hanging off the roof, off the side, off the back," Coby says. "He's coming in through the sunroof. I mean, every time the van came back in, there was a new hole to patch before I'd send it out again."

But maybe the most impressive feat of animation is the sequence in which the zombies first burst from the ground. The sequence calls for the earth to explode up into the air as the zombies emerge. In one early breakdown meeting, everyone more or less assumed this would be done after the fact with CG. But as special effects guru Brian Van't Hull points out, "Travis Knight wasn't in that meeting. He took a look at that scene and said, we'll do that in camera." In moments like this, the pride the team takes in having a CEO who is also a dedicated, respected animator is evident. He inspires people, as corny as that may sound. Yes, the directors are in charge, but when you know that somewhere out on the stage the big boss is behind a curtain, sweating the details, it's maybe a little easier to give your best effort. It's a spirit you can feel running through the place.

And for this scene, the riggers came through; they built the ground from foam rubber fitted together like a puzzle with each individual piece, some no bigger than a quarter inch across, connected to a pin or a screw or an actuator so that Travis could close that curtain on the world and animate an explosion, one frame at a time—a stunning stop-motion achievement.

As Knight has said, "Every bit of life you see up there on the screen has been sucked out of some animator." And it is tempting to think of the animator as a kind of lone hero, working in seclusion to bring these puppets to life. But when he sends the riggers and grips away and closes those curtains, all around him is the work—months and months of work—of a huge team spread throughout this rambling building. Nelson Lowry's art department has sweated over that set; there's Coby's van; there's Deb's jumper on Courtney; look at the way the zombie's jaw drops at the turn of a screw hidden beneath the hair Jill Penney made, in a pool of light that Matt DeLau devised; and all of it poked at and pondered over and perfected by directors Fell and Butler. One word into the walkie-talkie and here comes a model maker to patch a broken hand, a rigger to support a stumbling puppet, a painter to repair a smudge or smear. The animator works by himself but never on his own.

125

Ingenious rigging makes the earth (and everything else) move for *ParaNorman*.

Every rig and mechanism seen here will be painstakingly deleted from each frame of the finished movie.

128

Alan Cook • pen and ink

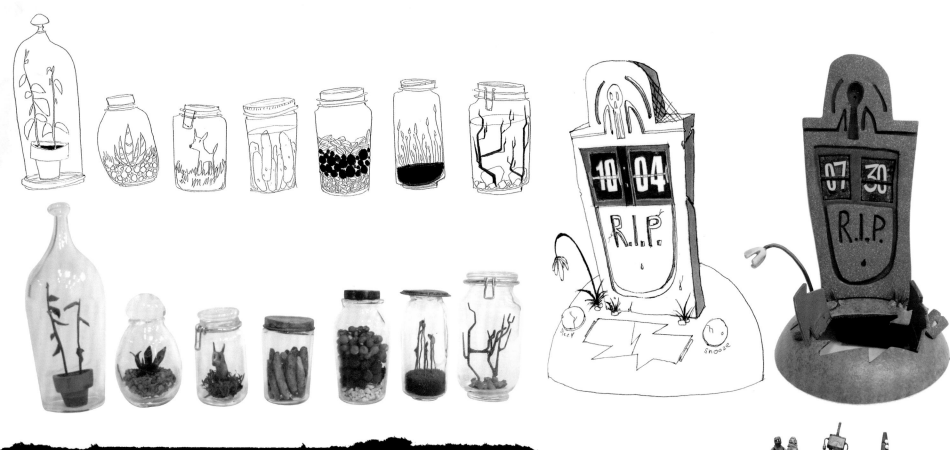

129

Alan Cook * pen and ink

"Chris's script described Blithe Hollow and its people as being tatty and rotten at the edges. It was really exciting to make a film in a world that wasn't really elegant or beautiful. It felt like we could break some new ground and find something unique for our film. It's kind of a given that if you take some charming vintage car or beautiful piece of Victorian furniture, stylize it, and make it in miniature, then it's going to impress people. But what happens if you put all that love and attention into a boring old chain-link fence or an ugly plastic air-con duct?"

—SAM FELL

131

Nelson Lowry • digital

Pete Oswald • digital

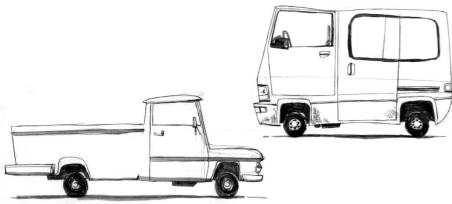

Ross Stewart • pen and ink

Stylized vehicles in various stages of design and construction.

It takes precision and skill to make a van look like its ready for the junkyard.

Ross Stewart • digital

Ross Stewart * digital

The "greens" branch of the art department is responsible for everything that grows in the *ParaNorman* universe, from trees and bushes to individual blades of grass.

Ed Juan • digital

Pete Oswald • digital

136

Ean McNamara • digital

Alice Bird • digital

Ed Juan • digital

Ed Juan • digital

Dave Vandervoort • digital

Alan Cook • digital

137

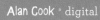

Alan Cook • digital

Ed Juan • digital

"There's a lot of stuff that I'm really proud of. The van chase. The mob scene on Main Street. Jeff Riley is doing some amazing stuff in Mr. P's study dragging dead Mr. P around. . . . But Travis's graveyard sequence is amazing —I've never seen anything like this, nothing as intricate, detailed, and beautifully realized as that."

—BRAD SCHIFF

Behind every stage of production is an army of talented artists and craftspeople.

"Animating on this film is the scariest thing I've ever done. It's the most intense, straight-in-the-deep-end animation. The style of animation we're doing, it blows my mind. The process of learning the personalities, the characters, how the puppets move . . . Every new puppet you're given feels like you've never animated before."

—JASON STALMAN, animator

Organized chaos fills every beautifully designed corner of Mr. Prenderghast's house (left),
as well as every creative corner of the LAIKA studio (above).

"The great thing about stop-frame is that you're shooting real things in real light with real lenses. Every frame can be unique. It's close to live action in that way. We wanted our world to be pushed in its shapes but have real and subtle textures. The character's faces especially needed delicate changes in skin tone and to react to light in a more translucent way than before."

—SAM FELL

# Bringing It All home

## Special effects and finishing touches

HAVING NOW MADE A FAIRLY EXTENSIVE TOUR of the vast
LAIKA building, missing nothing but the canteen populated by chatting
coworkers and recovering animators, and the halls of the production team, with
the impossibly complex whiteboards charting every shot and every unit in glo-
rious, color-coded detail, we make our way outside for a short walk across the
street, with just enough time to take a few breaths of fresh air before entering into
another building. The atmosphere is hushed, almost reverent. Here, in contrast
to the hands-on feeling that pervades LAIKA's workshops, a monitor dominates
every desk and the computer is king.

This is *ParaNorman*'s digital effects group, run by the venerable effects
guru Brian Van't Hul, or BVH as the directors refer to him, with such frequency
and confidence one could be forgiven for imagining BVH was a department or a
fancy technique, as in "I see some strobing—BVH can fix that."

Brian Van't Hul is a stop-motion fan and has been one forever. For some
people, the world of CG movies and digital effects is in direct opposition to the
crafty, artistic world of stop-motion—the Dark Empire vs. the scrappy rebels, if you
will. Brian doesn't see it that way. After all, a stop-motion film is one giant special
effect—ninety minutes of making inanimate objects come to life through the
expert application of certain techniques.

"I started out in stop-motion," says Van't Hul. "I worked with some of these guys on *Nightmare Before Christmas* and *James and the Giant Peach*. Then I took a hiatus from stop-motion and did a lot of live action. Then this project came up: It was a chance to get back to stop-motion, an opportunity to work with these guys I know, and a chance to get back to Portland. I jumped at it." The hiatus Van't Hul mentions corresponds to a fifteen-year career spent pushing the envelope of CG effects on some of the biggest blockbusters ever made.

According to Van't Hul, his job, as laid out for him by Travis Knight, is to use all his powers and skills to take stop-motion to the next level. "There are two very specific ways I'm expected to raise the bar: create background crowds and create set extensions."

In stop-motion, as we've seen, big crowds of characters are a challenge for a couple of reasons: time and money. The models are expensive and time-consuming to build, for starters. But the real time-suck comes when an animator has to animate the scene. Tracking and manipulating lots of background characters is prohibitively complex. "Sometimes you'll see people try to fake it with puppets that don't move. They're just stuck in the background like filler," Van't Hul says. "It works OK, but if you go to a higher angle, you see all these gaps." BVH and his team can put dozens of characters into a scene—hundreds, if necessary—that part is easy. The challenge is, as it always is for CG artists, to make these creations look realistic—only now the definition of what's realistic has changed. These characters need to belong to an unreal world—the world of *ParaNorman*—with all its special quirks and qualities.

"To do that," Van't Hul says, "we work very closely with the art and puppet departments to latch on to the design process they've been through with the characters. We say, 'What do you want these characters to look like?' And they might show us old characters or rejected characters. They might show us sketches, sculpts of rejected body parts—anything for inspiration. We'll get all that stuff, get design buy-off and then model it digitally."

"One of the first conversations I have to have with any new CG artist coming in is, 'Yes, we are doing photorealistic visual effects, just like a live-action film, but we have to be mindful of the puppet scale of things,'" Van't Hul continues. "One of my guys might paint a sweater and think, 'Wow, that's perfect.' And it might be, in the real world, but in this world it's too fine. The

**"I think what we're doing here is honest. The story has an emotional honesty to it that doesn't pull any punches. The characters are real. They move and talk and emote like real people. The place is not fantasy. It could be your hometown, warts and all, and the trash in the gutter has been given just as much care and attention as the white picket fences."**
**—CHRIS BUTLER**

model makers couldn't do that, so it looks fake." It is an adjustment comparable to speaking a new dialect of a familiar language. It requires a change in mindset but soon everyone gets it and it feels like second nature.

Once the characters are looking good, they need to start moving, and here again the same rule applies. "My guys can press a button and apply physics and make a character behave like it would in the real world. But the challenge is to make it walk and move like a puppet," he says. According to Van't Hul the directors will sometimes look at a sequence and say, "That's too smooth—it feels CG." So his guys will make a few frames stick and rough it up a little until it feels right. Meanwhile the stop-motion animators are always striving for absolute smoothness. "Sometimes I'll see a sequence they've done and it's perfect—totally perfect—so I'll say, 'Hey, that looks CG. You want me to go in and kind of rough it up for you?'" Van't Hul remarks. "Of course, they don't. It's pretty funny."

The second challenge for Brian's team is to digitally extend the sets. A stop-motion set is, by its nature, limited in scale. It is prohibitively expensive to build, light, and populate a large landscape. DP Tristan Oliver explains, "Normally, if you want the set to extend to the horizon, you could get by with a painted backdrop. And that works reasonably well in 2-D. But as soon as you add the stereo effect, you feel the flatness of the wall." The CG department was charged with extending *ParaNorman*'s many exterior shots so that you could see to the next hill and the next and the next. "Honestly," says Oliver, "I envisaged the special effects being a mess. But they've done a stunning job.

Ross Stewart • digital

Trevor Dalmer • digital

Ross Stewart • pen

> ## "Sometimes I hear people say, hey, we can do that in post—that's easy. But that's missing the point. An animator can do that on stage and it will look a hundred times more authentic."
> ### —BRIAN VAN'T HUL

I like to do as much in camera as I can. I don't like enhancement for its own sake, but this added value is really, really great. They absolutely adhere to the stylistic feel of the real sets."

Apart from creating crowds and extending sets, CG plays a big role in augmenting some of *ParaNorman*'s more paranormal aspects. For example, the very dramatic sky that swirls ominously over Blithe Hollow is a CG effect, but one based on a practical design. "The directors loved this material called *tulle*," Van't Hul explains. "It's basically bridal veil material." The rigging department engineered an articulated, expandable, swirling twister of tulle, which BVH's team then modeled. "It's not hard to make a CG version of that stuff," says Van't Hul, "until you have to make it move. The real challenge is to get it swirling and still have it feel like tulle."

Of course, Van't Hul's team is also responsible for all the work that normally comes with a stop-motion production—dealing with all the neck seams on the models and getting rid of the many wires, pins, and posts the riggers use to defy gravity. It has become a lot easier and cheaper and faster to do this kind of cleanup work compared to how it was a decade ago, but there is still an ethos in the rigger community of doing what can be done in-camera, using the set and the rigger's creativity to hide supports when possible. As Tristan Oliver so succinctly puts it, "Brian's job is quite big enough already without fixing stuff that we are too lazy or stupid to manage."

"We want to do things that look slick," Brian says, "But there is a visceral character to stop-motion we need to capture. Sometimes people ask me,

'Isn't CG easier? Why would you ever make it in stop-motion when you can just CG it?' That's like asking why would an artist paint a portrait when you could just take a snapshot. When you have a great crew, the results are more satisfying." From this it's clear that LAIKA has found exactly the right guy to head its effects department—someone of tremendous talent and ingenuity but also with the desire to use that talent to further the art of stop-motion, not supplant it. And it is just like LAIKA—this big warehouse full of crafty, hands-on-artisans—to not merely accept the high-tech aspect of CG as part of the process but to embrace it and, in fact, to push it to its limits.

It's hard to imagine assembling a better crew than the one LAIKA has put together for *ParaNorman*—full of immensely creative and experienced industry professionals as well as inspired and inspiring new talents, led by a directing team that reflects some of that same dynamic, with the veteran Sam Fell and the first-time director Chris Butler. Together they have imagined and improvised and engineered their way to realizing all the audacious goals Butler built into the script—the host of characters, the technically challenging mob scenes, the powerful action sequences, the expansive outdoor scenes, the surreal moments of supernatural magic.

In the end, it is all about the story. "The story Chris Butler told in *ParaNorman*," says Knight, "is about a group of outcasts who band together and use their individual skills to do something remarkable, something no one thought they could do, something they couldn't have done on their own. There's a reason we all gravitated to this story, because it's our story, too. It's LAIKA's story. We're a patchwork ragbag of misfits from all walks of life—but these are also some of the most talented people you could ever meet. And together, we're doing something amazing. We're taking the art of stop-motion filmmaking—this thing we've all loved and cherished since we were kids—and we're giving it a spark and vitality that has never been seen before. We started it on *Coraline*, we've taken it leaps and bounds on *ParaNorman*, and we're learning stuff every day that we will bring to the next film. That's what LAIKA is all about—a company and a community dedicated to pushing the boundaries of the medium and to making stop-motion filmmaking as wondrous as it can possibly be."

"When we came to the epic finale of the film, we needed to blow the whole world up and have Norman face off with the witch in an abstract spectral environment. Nelson [Lowry] made a dimensional tornado out of an old tutu which reminded me of the Wizard of Oz. Ollie Jones rigged it up with fishing wire and a lazy-Susan from a kitchen shop. I love that meeting of high and low tech you get at LAIKA."
—SAM FELL

Nelson Lowry • digital

Ben Adams • mixed media

Ross Stewart • digital

Ean McNamara • fabric

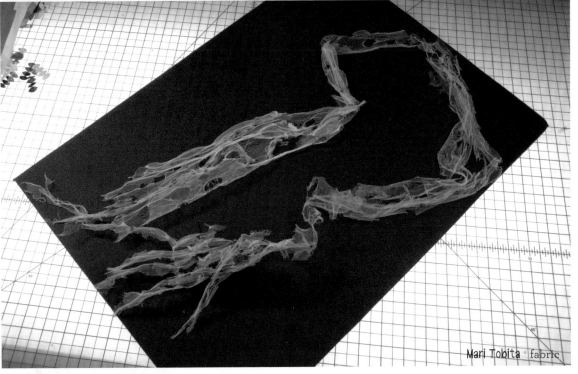

Mari Tobita • fabric

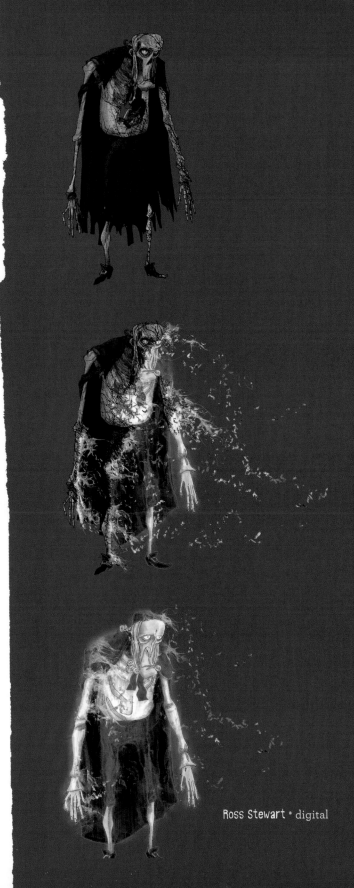

Ross Stewart • digital

"I've never seen stop-motion animation as nuanced, thoughtful, and restrained as some of the performances in this movie. We aspired to another level of acting, and these guys have surpassed it."
—CHRIS BUTLER

# Acknowledgments

I WOULD LIKE TO THANK everyone at LAIKA for giving me a glimpse into their amazing world, the folks at Chronicle Books for helping me so much with the writing, and my darling wife Tanja for absolutely everything else.

—JED ALGER

THE FILMMAKERS AND CREW AT LAIKA would like to thank Emily Haynes, Michael Morris, Becca Cohen, Beth Steiner, and Barbara Genetin at Chronicle Books for editing, designing, and producing such a gorgeous book. Designer Cat Grishaver deserves a big thanks for organizing hundreds of photos and files into a terrific layout and design. Thanks to Jed Alger for a thorough and insightful manuscript. And at LAIKA, thanks to everyone who has touched the book in its development, but especially to Nelson Lowry, Jenny DiMartino, Kathy Radcliffe, Martin Pelham, Reed Harkness, Rosemary Colliver, Tristan Oliver, Brad Schiff, Rob DeSue, Joseph Kortum, and Jason Ptasek.

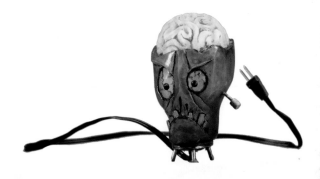